Reflecting Forewords

Praise for this book

'This book offers a fascinating tapestry of reflections on different themes at the centre of Robert Chambers' work over many decades. As a conversation between Robert and many diverse collaborators, the book provides an important commentary on many of today's big challenges for development. The book is a real treasure trove of interesting insights – a must-read for anyone interested in poverty, power, participation and progressive change.'
    Ian Scoones, Institute of Development Studies and co-editor of 'Revolutionizing Development: Reflections on the Work of Robert Chambers'

'A creative and unique collection which offers a fascinating journey through four decades of development thinking and practice. Readable, enjoyable and insightful!'
    John Gaventa, Professor, Institute of Development Studies

'Robert's forewords reveal his deep humanity, concern for those that are systematically excluded from social and economic processes that are central to their survival, and keen awareness of the human generated systems that generate these inequities. Yet they also reveal his awareness of how outdated worldviews and paradigms favor the status quo, are hidden in plain sight in the form of "normal professionalism" and how they can be disrupted through critical participatory methodologies. Most importantly, his forewords reveal his own humility and constant recognition of what he doesn't know and needs to learn, which gives us as readers permission to "not know" so that we might learn and give space for others to know. After giving Robert a cartoon zine recently that was inspired by his influence on my practice, perplexed, Robert asked me the question "does it self-spread, can it self-spread?" While I will bring this beautiful challenge to my work moving forward, I can say that indeed his ideas do and will continue to self-spread through this volume, as those of us who have had the privilege to know him and his ideas, will continue to take them forward through our community engagement praxis.'
    Alfredo Ortiz Aragón, Co Author of Action Research, 5th Edition (with Ernie Stringer)

Reflecting Forewords

Edited by
Robert Chambers and
Tessa Lewin

Practical Action Publishing Ltd
25 Albert Street, Rugby,
Warwickshire, CV21 2SD, UK
www.practicalactionpublishing.com

© Tessa Lewin, Robert Chambers and contributors, 2024

Tessa Lewin and Robert Chambers have asserted their right under the Copyright, Designs and Patents Act 1988 to be identified as General Editors of this work.

All rights reserved. No part of this publication may be reprinted or reproduced or utilized in any form or by any electronic, mechanical, or other means, now known or hereafter invented, including photocopying and recording, or in any information storage or retrieval system, without the written permission of the publishers.

Product or corporate names may be trademarks or registered trademarks, and are used only for identification and explanation without intent to infringe.

A catalogue record for this book is available from the British Library.

A catalogue record for this book has been requested from the Library of Congress.

ISBN 978-1-78853-406-2 Paperback
ISBN 978-1-78853-407-9 Hardback
ISBN 978-1-78853-408-6 Electronic book

Citation: Chambers, R. and Lewin, T. (2024) *Reflecting Forewords* Rugby, UK: Practical Action Publishing http://doi.org/10.3362/9781788534086

Since 1974, Practical Action Publishing has published and disseminated books and information in support of international development work throughout the world. Practical Action Publishing is a trading name of Practical Action Publishing Ltd (Company Reg. No. 1159018), the wholly owned publishing company of Practical Action. Practical Action Publishing trades only in support of its parent charity objectives and any profits are covenanted back to Practical Action (Charity Reg. No. 247257, Group VAT Registration No. 880 9924 76).

The views and opinions in this publication are those of the author and do not represent those of Practical Action Publishing Ltd or its parent charity Practical Action.

Reasonable efforts have been made to publish reliable data and information, but the author and publisher cannot assume responsibility for the validity of all materials or for the consequences of their use.

Cover design by Katarzyna Markowska, Practical Action Publishing
Typeset by vPrompt eServices, India.

Contents

Foreword	ix
Melissa Leach	
Preface	xiii
Tessa Lewin	
Acknowledgements	xv
Introduction	1
Robert Chambers and Tessa Lewin	1
Foreword to *Imposing Aid: Emergency assistance to refugees* (1986) by B.E. Harrell-Bond	5
Reflections from Priya Deshingkar	7
Editorial introduction to IDS Bulletin *Vulnerability: How the poor cope* (1989)	9
Reflections from Naila Kabeer	18
Reflections from Keetie Roelen	20
Forewords to *Beyond Farmer First* (1994) and *Farmer First Revisited* (2009)	23
Reflections from John Thompson	30
Foreword to *South African Participatory Poverty Assessment* (1997)	35
Reflections from Keetie Roelen	36
Foreword to the Japanese translation (2000) of *Whose Reality Counts? Putting the first last* (1997)	39
Reflections from Rosemary McGee	41
Foreword to *The Myth of Community: Gender issues in participatory development* (1998) by *Irene Guijt* and *Meera Kaul Shah*	43
Reflections from Andrea Cornwall	45
Foreword to *Stepping Forward: Children and young people's participation in the development process* (1998) edited by Victoria Johnson, Edda Ivan-Smith, Gill Gordon, Pat Pridmore, and Patta Scott	47
Reflections from Michael Gibbons	48
Forewords to *Who Changes? Institutionalizing participation in development* (1998) edited by James Blackburn and Jeremy Holland, and *Whose Voice?* (1998) edited by Jeremy Holland	51

Reflections from Jeremy Holland   57

Foreword to *In the Hands of the People: Selected papers of Anil C. Shah* (2001)   59

Reflections from Sachin Oza   61

Foreword to the Japanese translation of *Participatory Workshops* (2003)   63

Reflections from Jo Howard and Patta Scott-Villiers   65

Draft foreword to *How to Design a Training Course: A guide to participatory curriculum development* (2003) by Peter Taylor   67

Reflections from Peter Taylor   67

Foreword to *The Ripped Chest* (2004) by Harsh Mander   69

Reflections from Harsh Mander   70

Foreword to *Exploring the Science of Complexity: Ideas and implications for development and humanitarian efforts* (2008) by Ben Ramalingam and Harry Jones with Toussaint Reba and John Young   73

Reflections from Marina Apgar   74

Foreword to *Seasonality, Rural Livelihoods and Development* (2011) edited by Stephen Devereux, Robert Chambers, Rachel Sabates-Wheeler, and Richard Longhurst   77

Reflections from Stephen Devereux   80

Afterword in *Who Counts?* (2013) edited by Jeremy Holland   83

Reflections from Jeremy Holland   90

Foreword to *Poverty and Development in China: Alternative approaches to poverty assessment* (2013) by Caizhen Lu   93

Reflections from Tami Blumenfield   94

Foreword to *Wellbeing and Quality of Life Assessment: A practical guide* (2014) by Sarah C. White with Asha Abeyasekera   99

Reflections from Rosalind Willi   100
Reflections from Jackie Shaw   101

Foreword to *Participation Pays: Pathways for post-2015* (2015) edited by Tom Thomas and Pradeep Narayanan   107

Reflections from Tom Thomas   108

Preface to *Can We Know Better? Reflections for development* (2017) by Robert Chambers   111

Reflections from Jamie Myers   115

Foreword to *Adventures in the Aid Trade: Forty years practising development in forty countries* (2020) by Richard Holloway   117

Reflections from Richard Holloway	118
Failing forwards	121
Tessa Lewin	121
Knowing better	121
Doing better – towards radical equality	122

Foreword

Melissa Leach

If a book of forewords is a first, then a foreword to a book of forewords surely is too, and of the forewords that I have written myself over the decades (which pale alongside the panache and sheer quantity of Robert's), this one is unique. In reflecting on how to write it, three areas come to mind – each worthy of congratulation and celebration, and each suggesting reasons why this book is important and deserves to be widely read.

The first concerns Robert's extraordinary contributions to development and development studies over many decades. This book documents them beautifully in distinctive ways that complement other recent collections, from the 2011 book edited by Andrea Cornwall and Ian Scoones, *Revolutionizing Development*, that we re-launched in fully open access form in 2021, to the 2023 special issue of the Institute of Development Studies (IDS) Bulletin edited by Stephen Thompson and Mariah Cannon, *Power, Poverty and Knowledge: Reflecting on 50 years of learning with Robert Chambers*. The ideas and sensibilities that Robert has brought literally track the history of development and have transformed it along the way. Many of these contributions have been entwined with those of the research, teaching, learning, and influence of the Institute of Development Studies over the more-than-five decades since he joined in 1972. Robert and his work have been absolutely central to the unfolding story of development and development studies during this period, and to IDS's place in it.

Robert allegedly wrote forewords only to works he liked and his forewords in this book track many of his key themes: rendered here as *Conceptualizing and practising development: Paradigms, concepts, and methodologies*; *Methodological innovations: Participatory approaches and methods*; *Rural development, poverty, livelihoods: Perceiving people's realities*; and *The primacy of the personal – the kinds of professionals and professionalisms that would best serve development*. But just as importantly, these forewords and commentaries reveal brilliantly just how and why Robert's work has been so influential, showing his insistence on being prepared to up-end one's preconceptions, to be open to thinking and doing differently, to attend seriously to the voices and perspectives of people marginalized by dominant forms of knowledge and power, and to challenge power relations in all their variety, all delivered through his unique combination of wit and wisdom. Robert's irrepressible style shines through brightly here; a style that has inspired myriad people involved with development in all sorts of ways around the world. I count myself lucky to be among them, over a time period that coincidentally matches that of this book – the first foreword here was written in 1986, the year I had the privilege of being Robert's research assistant in work challenging conventional wisdom about trees and livelihoods that shaped my own career in ways too numerous to recount.

The second area looks forward, embracing the editors' nice pun in the book's title. Or is it a proverbial Freudian slip? I've sometimes been invited to contribute 'forwards' to books and reports, tutting pedantically over the mis-spelling and grammar and then reflecting that a foreword should, surely, be forward-looking – a forward indeed. This certainly seems to be Robert's view, as the forewords collected here show, and in keeping with his insistence at events celebrating his achievements that it's only worth looking backwards in order to look ahead. This is true of all eras, and I share Robert's conviction that at any given moment it is worth learning from the past in order to inform and shape our presents and futures, and to avoid reinventing wheels – something that the development world has been remarkably inclined to do. Yet the current moment seems like a particularly prescient one requiring fresh, historically informed forward thinking. People and places are reeling amid what some are terming a 'polycrisis' of climate and environmental change, pandemics, conflict, economic crisis, inequities, and geo-political turbulence. We are all living through shifts in the politics of knowledge, truth, and trust in a world of deep uncertainties and digitalized information. Many of these dynamics are undoing 'development' in its broadest and simplest sense, as put so aptly by Robert, of 'good change'. They also reveal a world of disruption, contradiction, and uncertainty. Many of the tenets of 'normal' Development with a big D – the discourses and practices of the aid industry – no longer hold – if indeed they ever did. The idea that Development programmes can be designed in some places, usually by people and organizations with greater power and privilege, and then rolled out to others – always distasteful – now seems anathema indeed. In this context it is becoming clear that a radical recasting of development and development studies is needed, along with a reimagining of what is possible. Robert's ideas and practices and the debates he has catalysed – captured so well in this book – offer some vital pointers. They remind us of the importance of complexity, nimbleness, and adaptiveness; of participation, partnership, and co-design; of listening, humility, and constant questioning; and of the kinds of expertise and professionalism needed for the future. Conveying Robert's irrepressible sense of optimism, the forewords here also remind us that even when things seem dire alternative futures are possible, keeping alive a politics of hope.

Third, a foreword to a book of forewords surely needs some comment on its form. This is not at all a normal book (just as the professionals that Robert encourages are not 'normal professionals'). Rather, the editors have brought together some highly diverse contributions, juxtaposed in unusual ways. Each foreword is accompanied by a contemporary comment piece that situates the work now: some are short introductory pieces contextualizing the authors and their work, articulating if, how, and why the ideas are still relevant, and what has changed in that field, while others offer reflections on how particular pieces of work influenced their own work and ways of thinking and doing. These commentators are very diverse – scholars and practitioners from many places, disciplines, ages, and stages. Some know Robert personally, while others do not, and were chosen because of their engagement with the writers that Robert wrote the forewords for. A few comment on the forewords as well as the original works. The result is a book that reads as a kind of multi-layered conversation, full of the plural voices, emergent complexities, reflexivity, entangling of the personal with big-picture issues, and the healthy disrespect for conventional boundaries that Robert's work urges and exemplifies. In many ways reading it is a bit like having a conversation with Robert himself, and (nearly) as enriching, interesting, and fun as that is. I hope that many will read it, enjoy it, and learn from it, just as so many of us have from Robert himself.

So, thank you to Robert for decades of forewords and of inspiration, and thank you to the contributors and editors for creating this collection. Let's share it widely and keep the development conversation going – forward.

Preface

Tessa Lewin

As I'm sure is often true with projects of this nature, this one has taken rather longer than it should, mostly thanks to me. Robert and I had had several exciting conversations about his idea for a book of forewords, over the years. In June 2020, I suggested that several of us might take on some of the administrative burden of the book, to support Robert. As is his way, this somehow led to me being introduced to Practical Action Publishing as a co-editor. That was as the first Covid lockdown in England had just lifted; it seemed, momentarily, that things might return to normal. They did not. Perhaps because of this – a time characterized by the multiple juggling of home schooling, distressed students, and online lectures and meetings – I initially found the forewords manuscript difficult to access. I sought out a range of scholars to write short pieces that positioned Robert's forewords, or rather the texts that they introduced, within contemporary practice and scholarship, a dialogue between then and now. Many of these pieces ended up being authored by the people that Robert initially wrote the forewords for, a development that has made the project rather 'meta', and even more unusual in format than was originally envisaged. I hope you like it. Robert, I'm sorry it took so long!

Acknowledgements

Thank you to Jenny for multiple cakes, biscuits, and cups of tea, and your general good humour and sharp wit.

Thank you to Caroline, Kipp, Lily, Erin and Rolo for our family walks.

Thank you to Mariah Cannon for invaluable administrative, editorial, and moral support.

Thank you, Rosalind Eyben, for your extremely helpful review.

Thank you to Melissa Leach for supporting the book, and for your foreword.

Thank you to all the contributors for engaging so generously in this.

Introduction

Robert Chambers and Tessa Lewin

> 'It is a privilege to be alive at a time when so much that had previously been accepted without question is being challenged, and there is such exhilaration and liberation exploring new ideas, approaches and methods, values and behaviours.' Robert, in the preface to the special issue of Agricultural Systems, 'Learning for the future: Innovative approaches to evaluating agricultural research' (Chambers, 2003: 119).

As Cornwall and Scoones (2011: 18) note in *Revolutionizing Development: Reflections on the Work of Robert Chambers,* Robert's 'immense enthusiasm and unbridled optimism' have made him 'extremely effective in enlisting and mobilising people'. Those who have sought out Robert to introduce their work were no doubt aware of this. On hearing about this book and reflecting on what Robert's 'endorsement' afforded his working paper, Ben Ramalingam wrote to Robert,

> I believe the ideas were shared more freely and discussed more widely than they would otherwise have been – especially at an operational level, and by developing country researchers and practitioners in particular. It also kickstarted a series of reflections on complexity and development, hosted by me and with your support ... your foreword actually opened a lot of doors for serious development scholars and practitioners to take the ideas seriously, and helped to open up the debate. You also provided very valuable peer review feedback which helped to locate the paper more firmly in a development context. Finally, your dedication and willingness to come to each and every event we ran in the series provided a basis for the 'epistemic community' that emerged around these ideas (personal correspondence).

In the spirit of the forewords, this is a sourcebook for development practitioners that seeks to draw lessons from the past that are relevant for the future. Its contents include forewords written by Robert to books on a wide span of aspects of development. We have been struck by how often these lessons have slipped out of sight, and what a loss this has been, especially for young professionals. We do not need to reinvent the wheel. The forewords here have been chosen because the books which they introduce contain valuable insights to take forwards into the rest of the century. We anticipate that this collection will be of interest to development professionals generally, and especially to teachers and graduate students of development studies, policy-makers, historians of development thinking and practice, activists, and those concerned with a better life for all. We know of no other book like it.

Most of the forewords included summarize the main lessons from the books they introduce. Each foreword is accompanied by a commentary piece situating the authors and their work in the field. Some articulate why these ideas are still relevant and in what way. Others reflect on how these ideas influenced their own work.

Reflecting Forewords is unashamedly ambitious. In our world of dramatic, unforeseeable change, it seeks to draw lessons and present insights that we judge should not be ephemera but can contribute on a lasting basis to policy, practice, and research in the rest of our 21st century. Readers will draw their own conclusions. The orientation is forward-looking into our unpredictable future, stressing the need to be alert, in touch, nimble, and guided by reflexivity.

The contents are organized chronologically, to give readers a sense of where they sit in the development of the field. Across the selection of forewords we identified four broad themes, which emerged inductively: *Paradigms, concepts, and methodologies*; *Perceiving people's realities*; *The primacy of the personal*; and *Participatory approaches and methods*. They, perhaps not surprisingly, map loosely onto those articulated by Cornwall and Scoones (2011) in their book *Revolutionizing Development: Reflections on the Work of Robert Chambers*, with two exceptions. One of Robert's themes here, *Perceiving people's realities*, is *Rural development, poverty, livelihoods* in Cornwall and Scoones's framing, but, on close inspection, there is significant overlap in the contents. And, Cornwall and Scoones's (2011) fourth theme is: *The kinds of professionals and professionalisms that would best serve development*, whereas Robert's is *The primacy of the personal*. Again, there are strong resonances between these, and both are centrally concerned with individual accountability and agency. We have thus adopted and adapted their themes. Many of the forewords might sit comfortably in more than one of these themes, but together they indicate the priorities of Robert's work across this time period. The first foreword was published in 1986 and the last in 2020. Our short conclusion is based on reflections and conversations between Tessa and Robert during the editing of the book. The forewords/forwards pun is deliberate. We have resisted the temptation to spell forewords forwards, a hybrid spelling used by some correspondents.

The themes

Conceptualizing and practising development: Paradigms, concepts, and methodologies.

Paradigms are thought of as interlinked and mutually reinforcing tendencies in concepts, principles, methodologies, behaviour and attitudes, and relationships, these all feeding into and sustained by mindsets. They are characterized diagrammatically as polar tendencies between a Newtonian paradigm for things, and a complexity paradigm for people. Too often in development praxis, methodological tendencies have moved towards top-down mechanistic requirements which misfit the unpredictable complexity of the realities they are operating in. The forewords that speak to this theme often challenge the binary between Newtonian and complexity paradigms.

Ben Ramalingam and Harry Jones's 2008 working paper, *Exploring the Science of Complexity: ideas and implications for development and humanitarian efforts*, articulates the complexity paradigm. They identify 10 concepts of complexity science, all significant, but some of which have slipped out of focus. All may be needed for understanding and action in the 21st century.

Jeremy Holland's book *Who Counts?* suggests the methodological win–wins that can come from work that combines qualitative and quantitative approaches. It celebrates the use of participatory methods to generate statistics. It documents processes in which facilitated, local participants are empowered through the statistics they generate, and outsiders gain through the insights generated, while all gain from the rigour and quality of the resulting data. There is a best of both worlds.

Stepping Forward: children and young people's participation in the development process (1998) gives reason for hope. The book shows again and again that children are capable of more than adults tend to recognize. The message to take from the book is that 'if we adults can only change our views and behaviour, children will astonish us with what they can do, be and become, and how in time they can make our world a better place.'

Methodological innovations: Participatory approaches and methods

Over the past 40 years participatory approaches, methods, and methodologies have blossomed and diversified. It takes an effort of imagination to appreciate what it was like in the 1960s and 1970s without them. The Farmer First conference and book *Farmer First: Farmer innovation and agricultural research* (1989) drew from the work of those who were pioneering learning from and with rural people at that time. This led to its successor conferences and books *Beyond Farmer First: Rural people's knowledge, agricultural research and extension practice* (1994) and *Farmer First Revisited: Innovation for agricultural research and development* (2009). The recognition of the importance of institutionally embedding participation was accompanied by a wider recognition of its challenges, successes, and failures, as illustrated by *Who Changes? Institutionalizing participation in development*. Seeing the need to go upstream, VSO commissioned Peter Taylor to write *How to Design a Training Course: A guide to participatory curriculum development* (2003). Translations of some of the literature into Japanese gave Robert an opportunity to summarize what had happened in the 1990s and 2000s in new introductions to the overview book *Revolutions in Development Inquiry* (2008), to *Whose Reality Counts?* (1997) with its themes drawn from the experiences of Participatory Rural Appraisal, and to *Participatory Workshops: A sourcebook of 21 sets of ideas and activities* (2002). Practical examples from numerous sources are presented in the defining book *Who Counts? The power of participatory statistics* (2013). Finally, *Participation Pays* (2015) is an inspiring account of experiences of Praxis in India. These show the rich diversity and potentials opened by participation when facilitators are creative and participatory, backed by organizations with participatory practices and cultures.

Rural development, poverty, livelihoods: Perceiving people's realities

Recent decades have seen transformations in the approaches, methods, and insights we privileged professionals have to hand to help us know the realities of those who are poor, vulnerable, marginalized, stigmatized, deprived, physically weak, and powerless. Barbara Harrell-Bond, in *Imposing Aid: Emergency assistance to refugees* (1986), set an example by living and learning in refugee camps in Africa. *The Myth of Community: Gender issues in participatory development* (1998) brought gender and participation together as never before. *Seasonality, Rural Livelihoods and Development* (2011) showed how multiple seasonal deprivations and professional seasonal blindness combined to sustain a blind spot. *Whose Voice? Participatory research and policy change* (1998) brought together the new methods of Participatory Rural Appraisal (PRA) in dramatic learning of new ways of enabling 'lowers' to present their realities to those in power through Participatory Poverty Assessments (PPAs). Over a hundred PPAs followed, in many countries, over the following years. One example is the *South African Participatory Poverty Assessment* (1997). The editorial introduction to an IDS Bulletin, *Vulnerability: How the poor cope,* distinguished vulnerability from poverty with which it had often been treated as synonymous.

The primacy of the personal – the kinds of professionals and professionalisms that would best serve development

This final theme emphasizes that to achieve good change and the inclusive universal justice that we seek demands and depends on personal action, and the accumulation of many individual actions. Examples follow from the life and work of two activist development professionals. Richard Holloway's *Adventures in the Aid Trade: Forty years of practising development in forty countries* (2020) is a rich harvest of diverse experience and practical learning. In India, Harsh Mander's commitment, empathy, and patient listening gave us two deeply disturbing accounts of what he learned in *Unheard Voices: Stories of forgotten lives* (2001) and *The Ripped Chest* (2004). *In the Hands of the People: Selected papers of Anil C. Shah* (2001) will stand as an enduring inspiration for all professionals, showing what can be done through a person's life-long commitment to those who are poor and marginalized.

Foreword to *Imposing Aid: Emergency assistance to refugees* (1986)

B. E. Harrell-Bond

> *Dr Barbara Harrell-Bond (1932–2018) was a legal anthropologist who founded the Refugee Studies Centre at the University of Oxford in 1982. She was involved in setting up legal aid services for refugees and research programmes in refugee studies in Uganda, Egypt, South Africa, and the UK. Imposing Aid: Emergency assistance to refugees is considered a seminal text in this field. It is based on a critical, in-depth study of the Ugandan refugee population in southern Sudan, who left Uganda in the wake of the overthrow of Idi Amin's regime.*

The intractable problem of millions of refugees, displaced persons, and victims of famine in rural Africa will not go away. The famines of Ethiopia, Sudan, Chad, and other countries in 1984 and 1985 have attracted attention as sudden emergencies but underlying them are long-term trends. Even on an optimistic view, the future prospects in Sub-Saharan Africa are appalling. Over the past two decades, the numbers of political refugees have grown from hundreds of thousands to millions. To these are now added millions who move en masse in distress because of loss of livelihood and starvation. Population in Sub-Saharan Africa is projected to grow by 3.0 per cent per annum for the next two decades, with a doubling time of some 24 years. The rural populations, after allowing for large-scale rural to urban migration, may rise by at least 50 per cent during the same period. On top of this, environmental degradation is widespread, with soil erosion, deforestation, and desertification. For tens of millions of rural people, economic decline, political instability, and ethnic tensions promise a worse future. Even if the rainfall failures of the early 1980s prove exceptional, the next two decades will probably see more, not fewer, crises, involving more, not fewer, people in the terrible decision to leave their homes and flee, destitute and desperate, from fighting, persecution, and famine, in search of safety, shelter, and food. At the same time, deeper indebtedness and the poverty of African Governments, less land for agricultural settlement, and fewer work opportunities in downwardly spiralling economies, will make it harder to host and help refugees, and harder for refugees to help themselves.

Despite the scale and awfulness of these forced mass migrations, there has been little systematic study of rural refugees and rural refugee relief work in Africa or indeed elsewhere. Until recently, refugee studies itself has not been recognized as a subject. Most books and papers on refugees and refugee programmes have had urban and elite biases to the neglect of those – in Africa the vast majority – who are rural, less well-educated, and poorer. Until recently, rural refugees have rarely been the starting point or central concern of research: they have usually been noticed and mentioned only in passing and not as the primary focus. In consequence, debates on policy questions like the relative merits of organized agricultural settlements and self-settlement have not been well-informed. It has been easy to think of rural refugees as an undifferentiated, uneducated mass. The points of view of refugees themselves have not been well-represented. Nor have the attitudes, behaviour, and problems of those who work in humanitarian and government agencies been examined. On the positive side, able efforts have been made to consolidate and communicate professional knowledge, for example in the journal Disasters and in the excellent UNHCR Handbook for Emergencies. But the fact remains that at a time when unprecedented numbers of desperate people have been migrating, struggling to survive in or out of camps, and dying, we who are not desperate or dying have still been negligently ignorant of what is really going on.

Just how ignorant we have been, is exposed in this book. To my knowledge there has been no previous study like it. Conrad Reining, also in the South Sudan, was the first social anthropologist to see colonial officials as part of his field and write them up in his classic, The Zande Scheme. With Imposing Aid, Barbara Harrell-Bond has given us a successor from the same region but with differences. The period is post-colonial, the occasion the crisis of massive influxes of refugees from Uganda. The people in the field are the refugees, their Sudanese hosts, and the staff of voluntary, humanitarian, and Government agencies. The book is timely and immediately relevant. In a more leisurely tradition, Reining took ten years from fieldwork to publication; but in keeping with the scale, importance, and urgency of the issues, Harrell-Bond, with assistance from Oxford University Press, has taken a matter of months. The main fieldwork, as researcher and participant–observer helping in the administration of official programmes, was conducted in 1982–3; and several chapters also draw in the experiences and findings of a team of committed researchers from Oxford who spent two months in the area in 1984.

There is much here that will be seen as new. Many readers will, like me, be surprised and shocked at how much we have been wrong and how much we have to learn. Those concerned with food supplies, nutrition, health, planning, and implementation in emergencies, and management and administration of refugee and other relief programmes, will find much to ponder. Perhaps more important, though, are the changes of perception which are opened up. Refugees speak and show the vivid awfulness of their experience, the brutality, terror, and desolation. Stereotypes dissolve under the impact of examples. Rural refugees in Africa, so easily thought of as statistics, are revealed as intelligent, articulate, and different individuals. Like other human beings, only more so than most others, they suffer, struggle to survive, need their self-respect, and have to mourn their dead. Convenient myths that somehow rural Africans are different – less sensitive, less individual, less vulnerable to trauma than others – cannot survive this book.

No one will feel comfortable with this book. Much of it disquiets, not least the difficulties, conflicts, and shortcomings of voluntary, national, and international agencies. Even-handedly, Dr Harrell-Bond spares neither herself nor others in recounting what happened, what was said, what done and what not done. In a fine tradition of social anthropology, she has not only observed others, but also herself, and reported on her own fallible human reactions and behaviour as well as those of others. In doing this, she sets a standard of introspection and honesty for others to follow, and shows us at first hand, from within, some of the personal stresses and dilemmas of those who work in mass refugee situations, and the courage and commitment needed to deal with them. She takes us intimately into the relations of refugees, hosts, and voluntary and official organizations, laying bare realities which have to be faced in order to learn how to do better.

The danger is, though, that strong reactions will distract readers from learning and from pondering and acting on the many positive lessons of the book. One such reaction could be to blame organizations or individuals. An antidote is to ask how one would have behaved oneself in similar conditions, under similar stress. Another reaction is defensive. Some who work in voluntary, humanitarian, or government organizations may feel threatened by the critical self-examination which the book invites. Some may even be tempted to search the text for error to justify rejecting the larger lessons; but if they do so, they, and future refugees, will be the losers. And yet another reaction could be the most damaging: to condemn aid and urge its termination. Negative academics will find here plenty of grist to their mills. They will not lack bad incidents to feed destructive cynicism. They will find plenty to quote selectively to argue that it would be better to do nothing. But before reaching such conclusions, they should reflect: on the terrible suffering of so many; on how difficult it is for those who try to mitigate that suffering; and on how much worse things would be if nothing were done. Moreover, Dr Harrell-Bond is clear on this point. The sane and humane thing to do is not to stop aid, but to augment and improve it. Honest examination of reality, however unpalatable, is a necessary painful means to that end. The challenge of this book is to recognize, embrace, and correct error. The message is not to do less, but to do better.

Let me commend this book to all concerned. They are many: refugees, who speak through these pages with such eloquence and who may come to understand more about humanitarian agencies; academics, activists, and journalists concerned with mass deprivation and migration; and especially those involved in humanitarian work, whether in headquarters or the field, and whether in foreign or national voluntary agencies, host Government departments, bilateral aid agencies, or international organizations like UNHCR, UNICEF, WFP, FAO, or WHO. They in their turn may come to understand better both refugees and themselves, and to see themselves the other way round, in the refugees' eye view.

Imposing Aid applies most directly to refugees and rural Africa but its value and relevance is wider, touching the behaviour and attitudes of the development and social welfare professions and their clients generally, on the organization of relief, and on the survival strategies of those who endure extreme deprivation. For all those concerned with refugees and others who migrate in distress, this is more than essential reading; it is essential learning. To the new professionalism which refugees deserve from those, not themselves refugees, who work with and for them, this book is a major contribution.

Source: Harrell-Bond, B.E. (1986) Imposing Aid: Emergency assistance to refugees. Oxford University Press. Reproduced by permission.

Reflections from Priya Deshingkar

Priya Deshingkar is Professor of Migration and Development at the University of Sussex with an interest in South–South migration and refugee studies. Her multidisciplinary research draws on the fields of human geography, anthropology, and development studies and focuses on intersectional understandings of displacement, irregular migration, human smuggling, and trafficking. She has conducted collaborative empirical research across various country contexts in Africa and Asia including an ongoing three-year Economic and Social Research Council funded project on protracted displacement of Somali refugees in Ethiopia. She was greatly inspired by Robert Chambers' participatory research approaches and incorporated them in her PhD research at IDS in the 1980s.

Robert Chambers' foreword to B.E. Harrell-Bond's 1986 book *Imposing Aid: Emergency assistance to refugees* drew attention to the need for listening to refugee voices, the importance of recognizing their diverse experiences, and the challenges of providing them with assistance. These themes are all the more relevant today. Harrell-Bond's book was based on a case study of Ugandan refugees in southern Sudan, providing a relatively rare account of the lived experiences of refugees back then. Since then, the refugee crisis in sub-Saharan Africa has escalated with major exoduses from countries including Somalia, Democratic Republic of the Congo, Central African Republic, South Sudan, and Nigeria. South Sudan, which gained independence in 2011, has now become the source of the largest refugee exodus in sub-Saharan Africa since 2013, with roughly 2.4 million refugees, mostly in Uganda and Ethiopia. Such a shift from being a host country to a country of origin demonstrates the volatility of the refugee situation and the growing challenges for the international development community.

Chambers was prescient in predicting that host societies with their own developmental challenges would struggle to aid refugees; indeed, the experience of refugees in sub-Saharan Africa today is testimony to this struggle. The reality for refugees today is dwindling aid resources, hardening border controls, and decades of protractedness with no clear solution in sight. Chambers' call for more research on refugees has certainly been heeded: refugee studies has gained recognition as a field with empirical research in many country contexts. Although many countries have signed up to the 2016 Refugee Compact which aims to find effective solutions, the reality of the politics of border control means that millions of refugees continue to live in limbo, unable to work or integrate into host societies. Recent efforts have focused on such protracted displacement to understand refugees' strategies for mobility and overcoming the constraints imposed by restrictive policies (see for example the Global Challenges Research Fund Protracted Displacement Economies project at the University of Sussex). Emerging findings show the many ways in which refugees have contributed to receiving societies and the ways that they help each other. Continuing empirical research and advocacy may help to shift perceptions and lead to policies that work with refugees as partners, recognizing their potential rather than treating them as a burden and excluding them.

Editorial introduction to IDS Bulletin
Vulnerability: How the poor cope (1989)

This is, strictly speaking, an editorial introduction, and not a foreword, but we decided to ignore this distinction here and err towards inclusivity rather than accuracy. It is an introduction to a 1989 edition of the IDS Bulletin, *which is IDS's flagship in-house journal. The pieces in this edition were drawn from papers presented at a small workshop on 'vulnerability' that Robert convened the previous year.*

Vulnerability

'Vulnerable' and 'vulnerability' are common terms in the lexicon of development, but their use is often vague. They serve as convenient substitutes for 'poor' and 'poverty' and allow planners and other professionals to restrain the overuse of those words. Some precision can be found in the use of 'vulnerable groups' where this refers to pregnant and lactating women, to children, or to disadvantaged communities such as scheduled castes and scheduled tribes in India. More often, though, vulnerable is used simply as a synonym for poor.

Vulnerability, though, is not the same as poverty. It means not lack or want, but defencelessness, insecurity, and exposure to risk, shocks and stress. This contrast is clearer when different dimensions of deprivation are distinguished, for example physical weakness, isolation, poverty and powerlessness as well as vulnerability. Of these, physical weakness, isolation and poverty are quite well recognised, and many programmes seek to alleviate them; powerlessness is crucial but it is rare for direct action against it to be politically acceptable; and vulnerability has remained curiously neglected in analysis and policy, perhaps because of its confusion with poverty. Yet vulnerability, and its opposite, security, stand out as recurrent concerns of poor people which professional definitions of poverty overlook.

Vulnerability here refers to exposure to contingencies and stress, and difficulty in coping with them. Vulnerability has thus two sides: an external side of risks, shocks, and stress to which an individual or household is subject; and an internal side which is defencelessness, meaning a lack of means to cope without damaging loss. Loss can take many forms – becoming or being physically weaker, economically impoverished, socially dependent, humiliated or psychologically harmed.

Failure to distinguish vulnerability from poverty has bad effects. It blurs distinctions and sustains stereotypes of the amorphous and undifferentiated mass of the poor. Poverty is often defined by professionals for convenience of counting, in terms of flows of income or consumption. Anti-poverty programmes are then designed to raise incomes or consumption and progress is assessed by measures of these flows. Indicators of poverty are then easily taken as indicators of other dimensions of deprivation, including vulnerability. But vulnerability, more than poverty, is linked with net assets. Poverty, in the sense of low income, can be reduced by borrowing and investing; but such debt makes households more vulnerable. Poor people, in their horror of debt, appear more aware than professionals of the trade-offs between poverty and vulnerability. Programmes and policies to reduce vulnerability – to make more secure – are not, one for one, the same as programmes and policies to reduce poverty – to raise incomes.

Care is also needed because vulnerability and security start as 'our' concepts and are not necessarily 'theirs'. To correct and modify them to fit local conditions requires decentralised analysis, encouraging, permitting, and acting on local concepts and priorities, as defined by poor people themselves. To date, such analysis indicates that for them, reducing vulnerability and enhancing security are recurrent concerns. Moreover, in recent years, while conditions have improved for some people, hundreds of millions of others have become more vulnerable; through greater exposure to physical or political disaster or threat, through higher costs of meeting contingencies such as health expenditures, or through loss of assets through individual or widespread disasters which have used up their reserves, leaving them less able to cope with future needs and crises.

With concerns like these a workshop on vulnerability and coping was held at the Institute of Development Studies (IDS) in September 1988, leading to this IDS Bulletin. Some 20 people took part, about half of them reporting on recent fieldwork. The focus was at the household level, and the aims were to try to understand better the nature of vulnerability, how poor people cope with risks, shocks and stress, and what should be priorities for policy and research.

Unlike poverty, vulnerability lacks a developed theory and accepted indicators and methods of measurement. The articles in this IDS Bulletin provide ideas and material which should contribute towards developing these. Most directly, the first article, by Jeremy Swift (page 8), presents a critique of parts of Amartya Sen's entitlement theory, and then outlines a new analysis of vulnerability and security based on a classification of assets into investments, stores and claims. Investments can be personal – in education, training and capabilities, or physical – in things, such as housing, land shaping and the like; stores can be of food, or real value, or of cash savings; and claims can be on other individuals or on households, patrons, the government, or the international community. In this perspective, households have portfolios of investments, stores and claims which change over seasons and longer periods, and have strategies for using them to deal with different stresses, shocks and demands.

The next three articles, by Housainou Taal, Tony Beck and Judith Heyer, illustrate the diversity of actions and strategies of those who are vulnerable and poor. Taal, reporting on two villages in the Gambia, shows how the compounded risks and stress of low and uncertain rainfall, price fluctuations, variable access to markets, and adverse seasonal conditions, are met by a repertoire of cropping patterns, crop storage, reduced consumption, off-farm work, asset disposal and exploiting community and kinship ties. Beck, presenting findings from fieldwork in rural West Bengal, highlights four types of activity which are important for the poorest, but little studied and often overlooked. These are the use of common property resources, which includes gleaning, collection of fuel, and gathering wild foods; changing the patterns of eating and food preparation; sharerearing of livestock; and mutual support networks. Heyer describes the behaviours of landless labourers in a village in a South Indian district, finding that although all were constrained in their options for investment, and none bought land, the asset strategies of two social groups of the landless were strikingly different.

The following three articles are concerned with how vulnerability is linked with deprivation, ill-health, and malnutrition. These are examined at the household level and also within the household. From his fieldwork on river blindness in Guinea (Conakry), Tim Evans describes the effects on households over time of the onset of adult disability through progressive loss of sight, leading to extreme stress and privation and to death and dispersal of other household members. From her study of very poor households in an urban slum in Bangladesh, Jane Pryer finds a strong association of severe child malnutrition with the ill-health and inability to work of breadwinning adults. Jane Corbett then examines vulnerability to sickness, and the high economic costs to households of ill-health, including how sickness makes poor people poorer through delayed treatment, the costs of treatment, and loss of earnings.

The last two articles assess programmes of intervention. Alex de Waal bases a critique of famine food relief on his 18 months of fieldwork in Darfur, Sudan (1985–7), concluding that in that context food relief did limit impoverishment, but that it was not significant in directly saving lives – the immediate cause of excess mortality being sickness. Finally, David Nabarro, Claudia Cassels and Mahesh Pant describe the impact on households of an integrated rural development project in Nepal implemented over a five-year period, and argue for support to the complex and well-developed strategies of the poorest in coping with crises and with the annual food gap, stressing access to health, veterinary and credit services, and to off-farm work and markets.

Perspectives

These articles are distinguished from much writing on deprivation by being based on direct, personal field research, and the insights derived from patient and sensitive learning from those who are vulnerable and poor. The findings often do not fit normal preconceptions. They qualify and complicate our view of vulnerability and coping. They challenge stereotypes of the poor and of programmes to help them. Readers will identify their own perspectives among those presented. I shall pick out five which strike me as important, and which have implications for policy and research.

i. Poor people's priorities

The concepts of poverty which most influence policy are those of the rich, who assume that they know what poor people want and need. By emphasising income and consumption, they neglect other aspects. Nor should vulnerability and security be given more attention than they deserve, case by case. Poor people have many criteria of well-being and deprivation. It is the outsiders who simplify them down to one or two, or a few. In his re-survey after 20 years of two villages in Gujarat, N.S. Jodha (forthcoming) found that the households whose real per caput incomes had declined by more than 5 per cent were, on average, better off on 37 of their own 38 criteria of well-being. Besides income and consumption, they were concerned with independence, mobility, security and self-respect.

The view is common that the poorest 'live hand-to-mouth'. This simplifies and distorts. Besides food they have other priorities. Although their wants and needs are usually complex, some of what they express as priorities can be captured by the three words survival, security and self-respect. Significantly, Beck found, as did Jodha earlier, how much self-respect can matter to the poorest. Most of Beck's respondents said that loss of respect was worse than hunger.

Similarly, very poor people can show extreme tenacity in taking a long view and struggling through sacrifice to maintain the basis of their livelihood. De Waal found a woman in Darfur, on leaving her village in the famine, preserving millet seed for planting by mixing it with sand to prevent her hungry children eating it. The primary aim of famine victims in Darfur was to preserve the basis of their future livelihood. Their strategies, as de Waal points out, were 'antidestitution' rather than 'survival'.

ii. Strategies: complex and diverse

In the common stereotype, the lives of poor people are simple and uniform. The reality is often the opposite. The coping strategies of those who are poor and deprived vary by region, community, social group, household, gender, age, season and time in history. As the case studies illustrate, most poor people have strategies which are complex and diverse. There are some who seek a single source of support, like the chakkiliyans described by Heyer who for a time accept being at the beck and call of one master. But most poor people do not choose to put all their eggs in one basket. Rather they reduce risk, increase adaptability, and seek a degree of autonomy, by developing and maintaining wider options, through the ability and willingness of different household members to do different things in different places at different times.

The range of means which poor rural people use for subsistence, to maintain their livelihoods, and to cope with contingencies, is impressive. Some are obvious and well known: cultivation, herding large and small stock, labouring in agriculture, off-farm economic activities, mortgaging and selling assets including future labour, begging, theft, and the splitting, dispersal and migration of families. Others which are less visible, less well recognised and less studied, are mentioned in this IDS Bulletin. They include eating less and worse, deferring medical treatment and expenditure, exploiting common property resources (such as the wild foods of West Bengal and Darfur), and share-rearing. In addition, Taal, Beck, Evans and Pryer all mention mutual support. In the Bangladesh slum described by Pryer, some workers had a selfhelp sickness insurance, and mutual help was common among poor slum women but little talked about. Most of these activities are hard for outsiders to see, and easy to harm by policy interventions which are blind to them.

The investment strategies of the poor also vary. As Heyer found, education can be an unproductive investment for some, with high opportunity costs from children's earnings foregone. Nor did the poorest in her village buy land, partly because it would entail loss of mobility. Although their economic status was similar, the chakkiliyans and the panadis showed very different social and economic behaviour. More generally, poor people try to diversify their portfolio of assets, defined in Swift's inclusive sense to include investments, stores and claims, so that they can handle contingencies and bad times better and minimise irreversible loss.

De Waal's Darfur study also illustrates local diversity. The behaviour of rural people in Darfur during the 1984–5 famine does not correspond with normal outsiders' expectations. They returned to their villages in order to cultivate, walking away from relief food to re-establish the basis of their livelihoods. This can be interpreted partly in terms of two local conditions: a relative abundance of wild foods; and a low level of past contact with government, including no previous experience with relief food supplies. Famine behaviour in Northern Ethiopia is different: there, people are more inclined to move to roads in distress, having in the past been supported by government in crises. Part of the diversity of strategies derives thus from people's past experience, and in turn affects how best to intervene.

iii. Changing degrees of vulnerability

In parts of the rural South, trends can be discerned which make poor people more vulnerable. To be sure, where their incomes rise, they have the means to make investments, to build up stores, and to establish claims which make them less insecure. Where services improve, isolation and vulnerability diminish. Where tenure of land, water and trees is clearly vested in the poorer, they become more secure. But in some countries and regions, especially in sub-Saharan Africa, declining real incomes imply increasing vulnerability, and in addition, there and elsewhere, four trends with negative effects can be found.

The first is a decline in patron–client obligations. These are disliked more and more by clients who find them demeaning, and sought less and less by patrons, who prefer a cut-and-dried casual wage relationship to more open-ended responsibilities to dependent clients. Patterns here are not uniform; the South India case presented by Heyer is a partial exception where patrons paid relatively high wages to those who accepted labour attachments.

The second trend is declining support from the extended family. Not just in urban areas, the tendency is towards smaller consumption units, as noted by Taal in the Gambia, and towards the nuclear household. The weakening of wider family obligations then leaves households more exposed.

The third trend is rising costs of contingencies. Weddings, brideprice and dowry have tended to rise, except for the very poor and destitute who simply cannot afford them. Perhaps more seriously, medical expenses have risen. Whereas in the past, only relatively inexpensive indigenous medicine was available, many poor people now have access to more expensive allopathic treatment. A new form of impoverishing vulnerability is costly treatment for sickness which is not cured, as illustrated by the case history of Abdullah's family described by Pryer.

The fourth trend is localised, but severe in areas of recurrent famine such as the Sahel, where interventions to provide support for the vulnerable tend to come late. This is mortgage, sale or loss of tangible assets in order to obtain food, culminating in loss of means of livelihood and destitution. Many millions in sub-Saharan Africa, after the crisis of 1984–5 are more vulnerable than before, because they have used up or lost most or all of their tangible assets, and have so little opportunity to build them up again. In consequence, it now requires a less severe crisis to bring them to dependence on outside support.

These trends to greater vulnerability are not universal. But where they occur, they pose problems for policy. The question is whether and how the state and the international community should and can be open to claims which were formerly met by patrons, kin and the disposal of tangible assets.

iv. Assets, contingencies and livelihoods

Contingencies impoverish in different ways. Households have different strategies and exploit or cash their assets in different combinations and sequences.

Following Swift's separation of tangible and intangible assets into investments, stores and claims, the strategies of poor people can be seen as the management of a complex portfolio of assets, each with a different profile. The criteria of poor people themselves deserve empirical investigation, but some characteristics of tangible assets that appear important can be noted: on the positive side, divisibility, ease of sale or mortgage, and good price including avoiding a distress sale and maintaining value in bad times; and on the negative side, bad effects of disposal of assets can include loss of production, diminished value of labour power, and loss of self-respect. The strategies and sequences of coping with crises vary by household and by local conditions, but Corbett's (1988) comparative analysis of studies of four famines found that an early step taken by poor households when they see bad times coming is to change their diet and eat less, reflecting in part the priority they give to preserving those assets which provide their means of livelihood.

One view has been that while poor people have assets such as livestock, they should not receive support since they can sell them and so remain independent. In contrast, it can be argued that past crisis interventions have often come too late, after poor people have become poorer by disposing of productive assets, or after they have taken debts or obligations which prejudice their livelihoods, and that future interventions should come earlier.

V. The care of adult bodies

The main asset of most poor people is their bodies. General and measurable concepts like 'labour power', 'labour availability' and 'dependency ratio' blunt this sharp point, and miss the stark personal reality. The good ethical and humanitarian reasons for providing health services and reducing suffering from sickness sometimes serve to divert attention from the economic aspects of ill-health, analysed by Corbett. These include the plain facts that the poorer people are, the more it matters to be able to work and earn, the more they depend on physical work, and the higher are the personal costs of physical disability.

At the same time, the bodies of the poorer are more vulnerable than those of the less poor: they are more exposed to sickness from insanitary, polluted and disease-ridden environments both at work and at home, and to accidents in their work; they are weaker, with malnourishment and previous sickness tending to reduce resistance to disease and to slow recovery; and the poorer have less access to prophylaxis or to timely and effective treatment. Worse, in rural tropical conditions, these and other adverse factors usually combine in a seasonal syndrome during the rains when high exposure to infection, hard work in cultivation, food shortages, isolation, indebtedness and low access to health facilities, occur together and interact. The time when it most matters to be able to work is then also for many the time when they are physically weakest and most at risk.

Among the physical factors which impoverish, accidents have been neglected, yet many of the poor are exposed to disabling accidents. Rural activities such as quarrying, mining, fishing, hunting, building, brickmaking, ploughing, and herding, and urban activities – in factories, transport and construction – are often physically hazardous. The resulting accidents are rarely counted and little considered in the literature, yet again and again, individual case studies of destitute households reveal an accident as the event which impoverished – disabling an adult, especially a breadwinner. At a sudden blow, the body, the poor person's greatest and uninsured asset, is devalued or ruined. From being an asset, at one stroke it becomes a liability that has to be fed, clothed, housed, and treated. A livelihood is destroyed, and a household made permanently poorer.

Medical costs, too, can impoverish. Where treatment is sought, as Corbett and Pryer show, it often entails heavy expenditure until the household exhausts the tangible assets it can sell or mortgage. Where the treatment fails but the sick person survives, this leaves the household destitute and with a dependent adult to support. Once the household is assetless and chronically poor, the costs of any further treatment may be spread in only small amounts, which are then, as Pryer found, greatly exceeded by the earnings foregone from work lost through disability.

The importance to the whole household of the physical capacity of adults is highlighted by the studies of both Evans from Guinea, and Pryer from Bangladesh. Evans' model of the progression of river blindness in a husband shows appalling pressure placed upon other members of the household, leading to malnourished children and the early death of his wife. Pryer's finding – that households where an adult earner had been sick during the previous month were two and a half times more likely than others to have a severely malnourished child – carries the same implication. Much attention has been focused, correctly, on the health and well-being of women and children, and nothing should detract from that. But what we now see is that among the very poor the health of a breadwinner, whether male or female, is critical for the well-being of the rest of the household; and that preventing disability in breadwinners, or curing it, can also prevent malnutrition in children. Indeed, the cheapest way to prevent child malnutrition may often be to prevent adult sickness, and the most sustainable way to overcome the malnutrition of a child may often be to overcome the disability of an adult.

Implications for policy

The most general policy implication of these perspectives is to question our assumptions. In Heyer's words, 'what seems obvious is often wrong'. The solution is again and again to enquire of the poor what they want and need, and to strive to understand their conditions and how they cope. The answers will point both to interventions which enable them to be better off in their own terms, and, often, to a change of priorities and programmes.

For poor people, there are trade-offs between vulnerability and poverty or, to put it positively, between security and income. Some programmes, like the Integrated Rural Development Programme in India, seek to raise incomes but at the same time entail a loan and indebtedness. But poor people all over the world are reluctant to take debts which increase their vulnerability. One implication is, therefore, that government programmes which, whatever their benefits, make poor people indebted or in other ways more vulnerable, should be treated with caution. Such vulnerability can be reduced through group loans, and through insurance which covers the debt if the asset is lost. Reducing vulnerability can be as important an objective as reducing poverty.

More specific policy implications are presented in articles in this IDS Bulletin. Without summarising these, some which stand out are:

To investigate and treat each group and situation in its own right

This IDS Bulletin makes the point again and again that the conditions and strategies of poor and vulnerable people vary. There are practical limits to tailoring policy and action to individual persons, households or groups, and programmes targeted to the poorer are notorious for missing their targets and being captured by the less poor. Nevertheless, action can fit better when based on sensitive understanding of who are at risk, what they want and need, and how they cope.

To support diversification, security and current coping strategies

Labour shortages, sources of farm incomes, mobility, new economic niches opened up by economic growth, better marketing and prices for the produce of small farmers, access to services, cheap food, and a variety and abundance of common property resources, are all examples of conditions in which poor people stand to do better through diversification. Nabarro, Cassels and Pant stress the basic importance of economic growth, and of a range of inputs, services and welfare provision that can be used by households when they need them. Diversification of what is provided permits diversification of income sources and assets.

Support for current coping strategies can take many forms. In detail, much depends on local conditions and needs. When poor people's priorities, strategies and conditions are the starting point, the conclusions may not be conventional. Two examples arising from fieldwork in Mali are improving communications to areas where wild foods are abundant, and enabling poor people to buy food cheaper in bulk (pers. Comm. Susanna Davies).

To monitor vulnerability and act on asset indicators

Early warning systems are now many. As Swift points out, low assets would be good indicators of vulnerability. The question is whether it is feasible to monitor the assets and exposure of vulnerable communities and groups so that action can be triggered early enough to prevent or minimise further impoverishment at times of stress.

To put floors under the vulnerable

The Maharashtra Employment Guarantee Scheme provides a model of how, given the administrative capability to respond, poor people can be empowered to demand and receive work and remuneration when they need it. Food-for-work schemes require less sustained administration and can have the same effect – putting a floor under the poor to enable them to survive a bad time without having to become poorer. It seems more cost effective, besides more humane, to use such means to reduce vulnerability and prevent impoverishment than, once people are poorer or destitute, to try to enable them to recover.

Guaranteed markets at good prices for whatever poor people sell at bad times are another form of floor. The items sold vary locally, including livestock, poultry, firewood, charcoal and other tree products, and jewellery. Where people are going to sell these anyway, maintaining the prices they fetch can only help those who have to sell.

Cheap and accessible food is another form of floor. Whatever their defects, programmes such as Andhra Pradesh's cheap rice help the poorest, providing they have access to buying it. Assuring basic food at low prices is one of the safest ways of mitigating poverty and reducing vulnerability.

To improve fallback food

The neglect of famine crops and wild food in agricultural research promises scope for quick gains through the international transfer of germplasm, and for big gains from breeding. The need for a non-toxin variety of the fallback food kassari dal (*Lathyrus sativus*) is mentioned by Beck. In this case, a low toxin variety bred in Canada is being transferred to Ethiopia where other research is also going on. There are probably many similar opportunities, unexploited because famine and fallback foods have not until recently been considered important or of professional interest.

To stress even more the provision of effective health services free or at low cost

Health services which are cheap or free, and accessible and effective, emerge from studies in this IDS Bulletin as more important than ever. They have a greater role in reducing vulnerability and limiting impoverishment than has been recognised. Adult health, especially the health of breadwinners, is more important than many have supposed for the nutrition and health of children. Many considerations bear on the new fashion for fees and cost recovery as part of structural adjustment. But one point to stress in the debate is that charges for health services threaten to delay or deny treatment precisely to those who most need it, and to deter, hurt and impoverish those who are most vulnerable.

De Waal's Darfur study draws attention to the importance of protecting the health, especially of children, in famines. Relief food can have a vital part to play in reducing suffering and in preventing impoverishment, depending on local conditions; but de Waal's conclusion that in the 1984–5 famine in Darfur, the cause of excess mortality was sickness, not lack of food, points to the importance of immunisation, of clean water, and of enabling people to stay where they are instead of migrating to disease-prone concentrations in camps around towns.

In epidemics, to help not only sick adults, but also their dependants

In microcosm, Evans' study of river blindness in Guinea gives hints and clues for scenarios for AIDS in rural areas, as its acute phase becomes prevalent. River blindness differs in that those afflicted become disabled and die more slowly than with AIDS, and so are dependent for longer, but there are also strong similarities. With concentrations of acute AIDS, the progression of decline described by Evans for a household would affect whole communities, with rising dependency ratios, increased child labour (and withdrawal from schools), decreasing areas under cultivation, greater vulnerability to other diseases, declining capacity for mutual support, and out-migration by older children. In such conditions, the priority will be not just to care for the sick but to sustain the survivors, who will include the very old and the very young.

Implications for research

Policy for research is one key to better practice. Besides the articles which follow, recent empirical research (e.g. especially Rahmato 1987) has shed new light on vulnerability and coping. But much also remains to be known and understood. Some research priorities are indicated in contributions to this IDS Bulletin. Many more could be suggested. Among those that merit mention are:

- developing simple and sure methods for enabling poor people to analyse their conditions and identify their priorities;
- developing and testing indicators of vulnerability. These might include households' net assets, labour power, dependency ratios, access to food, and exposure to external stress and shocks;
- assessing the modes, costs and benefits of prevention rather than cure – of reducing vulnerability and preventing impoverishment compared with enabling recovery;
- assessing and comparing vulnerability and assets within households, between groups of people, and between regions and continents, and how these change over time, with special attention to (a) groups and areas where vulnerability increases, and (b) impoverishing costs of medical treatment;

- assessing and comparing coping strategies under stress, including sequences of response, thresholds between types of response, and the value and use of different sorts of assets;
- the effects of civil disorder (war, raiding, refugees, thefts, etc.) on vulnerability and coping strategies. This is a gap in this IDS Bulletin, and would include effects on both (a) the economic environment, including local markets and the quantity, quality, and reliability of supply, and cost of food and other basic goods for purchase or barter, and (b) household strategies, including farming practices, food storage and intra household availability and division of labour;
- relief and development policy, and the fit and effects of alternative relief policies and practices in different conditions and on different groups. This includes the relative importance for survival, limiting suffering, and sustaining livelihoods, of food relief, cash relief, cheap food including bulk purchase, food-for-work, fodder relief for livestock, employment guarantee schemes, small loans, purchase of tangible assets poor people sell at times of stress, health and medical interventions, and ways of strengthening and supporting people's present strategies for coping;
- the effects of adult disability and death on household viability, strategies and behaviour. This could build on the work of Evans and Pryer, and the longitudinal studies of Nabarro, Cassels and Pant, and would be of special relevance in regions where the acute phase of AIDS becomes endemic.

Conclusion

The conclusion has to be humility. Through the new insights from their fieldwork and analysis, the contributors to this IDS Bulletin show how ignorant, and sometimes how wrong, we in the development professions have been. Through local study and individual cases, they also show how varied is that universe of vulnerability and poverty for which we seek simple explanations and single solutions. Most who read these articles will feel unease at the confidence with which in the past we have combined ignorance with error. They may speculate too on how wrong we continue to be.

The lesson for the future is to enquire and question, doubting what we think we know, and learning from and with those who are vulnerable and poor, as contributors to this IDS Bulletin have done; and to do this, not once, not in one locality, and not for one group only, but again and again, in each place, and for each sort of person. For that is the surest path to better understanding, and to action that will better fit and serve the diversity of conditions and people and their changing priorities and needs.

References

Corbett, J. (1988) 'Famine and Household Coping Strategies', World Development 16.9: 1099–1112

Jodha, N.S. (forthcoming) 'Social Science Research on Rural Change: Some Gaps (A Footnote to Debate on Rural Poverty)', in Pranab Bardhan, Rural Economic Change in South Asia: Methodology of Measurement

Rahmato Dessalegn (1987) 'Peasant Survival Strategies', in Angela Penrose (ed.), Beyond the Famine: An Examination of the Issues Behind Famine in Ethiopia, Geneva: International Institute for Relief and Development, Food for the Hungry International

Chambers, R. (ed.) (1989) 'Editorial introduction: vulnerability, coping and policy'. IDS Bulletin 20(2), Brighton: Institute of Development Studies. https://bulletin.ids.ac.uk/index.php/idsbo/article/view/1821

Reflections from Naila Kabeer

> Naila Kabeer is Professor of Gender and Development at the Department of International Development and on the faculty of the International Inequalities Institute at the London School of Economics. She was at the IDS between 1985 and 2010 and had many interactions with Robert over the years. His reflections on the value of asking whose reality counts influenced her first piece of fieldwork after joining IDS and resulted in a methodology for monitoring poverty from a gender perspective. The influence was lasting and also explains the title of her first book: Reversed realities: Gender hierarchies in development thought.

The 1989 IDS Bulletin on Vulnerability came out of a workshop held in 1988 with around 20 participants. I was one of them, though to discuss rather than present a paper. Robert's introduction to the Bulletin summarizes the papers, all based on primary fieldwork, and pulls out some key themes. Let me focus on those which found their way into my own subsequent research. A first theme was the distinction between poverty and vulnerability, between the static, income-based understanding of poverty that underpinned the single headcount measure which was standard at that time, and the more dynamic conception of vulnerability which referred to the heightened risk of poor people to both generalized and idiosyncratic shocks that could plunge them into deeper poverty. A second was the importance of assets and claims to their ability to weather such shocks. If the static view tended to prioritize adequacy of income flows, the dynamic view added a focus on stocks of wealth and the nature of social relationships.

A third important theme was the importance of understanding poverty from the perspectives of the poor. Past research on such perspectives, Robert pointed out, had suggested the existence of a hierarchy of needs – survival, security, and self-respect. The latter, I would add, is often tied up with social standing within the community – how we are perceived by others. The point about this hierarchy was that it could often entail harsh trade-offs if poor people could only meet their need for survival or security in ways that undermined their self-respect – through reliance, for instance, on patron–client relationships that provided them with protection from the worst effects of crisis but required them to be at the beck and call of wealthy landlords for the rest of the time.

Very soon after the workshop I was commissioned by DANIDA, Bangladesh, to carry out fieldwork in order to bring a gender dimension to a poverty monitoring framework that was being developed by a research team in Bangladesh. Inspired by the workshop to seek out the perspective of poor men and women, I carried out several individual and group interviews in a number of field sites in rural Bangladesh.[1]

The framework I used, influenced by the need to distinguish between static and dynamic conceptions of poverty, was organized around a distinction between 'poverty as state' and 'poverty as process'. The central finding that came out of that research was that 'women experience[d] the state of poverty differently to, and often more acutely than, men and became impoverished through different processes'.

In terms of the 'state' of poverty, national statistics already provided data on gender differentials in health and nutrition, but my fieldwork pointed to how the daily diets of men and women from the same household might differ. The wages that men earned labouring in the fields frequently included the normal items of a basic daily diet in rural Bangladesh: rice, lentils, and perhaps vegetables. Denied the opportunity to work, women were more likely to rely on gathering 'poverty food', wild plants that grew in common property reserves.

The class-based analysis of poverty in the Bulletin highlighted the use of violence and harassment against the poor by wealthy rural power holders. It failed to highlight the sexual nature of the violence levelled against women from poor households by these same groups. Nor did it recognize the high incidence of domestic violence against women and children as male breadwinners took out their frustrations in failing to find work on vulnerable members of the household.

As far as the process of poverty was concerned, I pointed to the very different endowments available to men and women within the same household to withstand crises: the ability of men to walk away from dependent members in times of crisis in order to conserve their earnings for themselves, resulting in impoverished female household heads; and the greater reliance of poor women on the sale of their physical labour to look after themselves and their children in the absence of any wealth of their own. There was one other important finding that came out of that research. It related to the hierarchy of needs and the harsh trade-offs faced by the poor – but also how these played out differently for men and women. It was evident from my interviews how important it was to men's sense of self-respect to be seen to be discharging their roles as family breadwinner. Their success was judged by their ability to keep women from their households in respectable seclusion, confined to unpaid care work. I found that even men from very poor households sought to forbid their wives to take up public forms of wage labour because it implied their own failure as breadwinners. But these notions of social status and family honour were not a priority for many of the women I interviewed. As one put it:

> *What need have the poor for self-respect or propriety? Everything is dictated by scarcity (abhab): scarcity of food, scarcity of clothes, scarcity of shelter, there is no end to the scarcity … there are mothers who cannot feed their children, can they afford propriety?*

Her statement vividly conveyed the message that for those living on the margins of physical survival, the struggle to stay alive was an overriding priority. But it also contained the suggestion that for poor women, the notion of self-respect itself might be more closely tied to feeding themselves and their dependants than to cultural ideals of female propriety which would hamper their ability to do so.

PS: There was one other lesson, this time methodological, which I took away from this fieldwork and conveyed to Robert: it was very difficult to do group-based interviews in Bangladesh villages because everyone talked at once!

Reflections from Keetie Roelen

Keetie Roelen is Senior Research Fellow and Co-Deputy Director of the Centre for the Study of Global Development at the Open University, UK. Her research focuses on areas of poverty, social protection, and anti-poverty interventions in relation to children, women, and psychosocial wellbeing. She is a mixed-methods researcher, holding both quantitative and qualitative research skills. She first learned about Robert's influential work more than two decades ago, as part of a team undertaking a participatory poverty assessment in northern Namibia, before working alongside him at IDS for 12 years.

Vulnerability: old wine that needs a new bottle

In his introduction to the 1989 IDS Bulletin *Vulnerability: How the poor cope* (above), Robert highlighted that vulnerability and poverty are two very different things, and that they should not be conflated. Vulnerability isn't about a narrow focus on lack of income or material deprivation but compels us to think more broadly about how lives are shaped by the interaction between exposure to risk and defencelessness to shocks. Doing so, he argued, allows us to move away from oversimplified distinctions between the 'poor' and 'non-poor', and their inevitable stereotypes. It helps overcome misguided policy recommendations that fail to recognize people's complex web of strategies and relationships that act as a buffer for when things take a turn for the worse.

More than 30 years have passed since Robert's contribution, yet his call to pay greater heed to the issue of vulnerability has only grown more urgent. We don't have to look far to realize that vulnerability has become a defining feature of many people's lives. In the last three years, billions of lives were disrupted as a result of the Covid-19 pandemic. Millions experienced devastating effects of climate change, including rampant wildfires in Australia, widespread floods in Pakistan and devastating drought across Europe. Conflicts in Tigray, Ethiopia and in Ukraine rage on without a resolution in sight. As I'm writing this, towards the end of 2022, the cost-of-living crisis is squeezing household budgets and pushing many families to the brink of despair.

Being faced with multiple and interlocking shocks requires ingenious coping strategies, especially for those who are at the sharp end of the socioeconomic fallout of such shocks. Nevertheless, many policies remain blind to how people respond to vulnerability and endeavour to establish a form of security. Monocropping strategies force farmers to replace their multiple crops grown for own consumption with commercial crops, increasing their risk of hunger when harvests fail. Abolitionist child labour policies remove children from work without offering a viable alternative source of income, pushing them into poverty or hidden – and often more harmful – forms of work. Microfinance, once hailed as one of the most promising development interventions, has led to widespread indebtedness, thereby impeding entrepreneurial activity rather than supporting it.

With 2030 edging closer and debates about what is to come after the Sustainable Development Goals (SDGs) slowly taking shape, there is no better time to be reminded of the value of the concept of vulnerability. Moving the gaze beyond a narrow focus on poverty – be it monetary or multidimensional – allows for taking account of, and responding to, people's complex realities. In an era of socioeconomic, political, and environmental uncertainty at a global scale, vulnerability is a crucial lens through which to shape policies that truly change lives for the better.

Note

1. The results were published as an IDS working paper and an article in the *Journal of Peasant Studies*.

Forewords to *Beyond Farmer First* (1994) and *Farmer First Revisited* (2009)

> There are three Farmer First books, each an edited volume drawing on workshops held at IDS on innovative work in agricultural research. The first workshop in 1987, led to the publication of Farmer First *(1989), for which Robert wrote the introduction. The second workshop in 1994, led to the second book,* Beyond Farmer First, *published that year. The final workshop in 2007 produced the third book,* Farmer First Revisited, *in 2009. Spanning two decades, these three books build upon one another. Broadly speaking,* Farmer First *is about research on the farm, as well as the research station;* Beyond Farmer First *about power and the pluralism of knowledge; and* Farmer First Revisited *about an explosion of methods and partnerships. Robert wrote the foreword for the second and third book, both of which we include here.*

Beyond Farmer First *(1994)*

In July 1987, some fifty natural and social scientists met for five days at the Institute of Development Studies at the University of Sussex, UK, for a workshop on Farmers and Agricultural Research: Complementary Methods. The aim was to bring together professionals who had been involving farmers in the research process to share experiences and methods, to take stock and to plan for the future. The focus was on the resource-poor farming systems on which perhaps 1.4 billion people depended for their livelihoods. The papers and discussions were edited to become the book *Farmer First: Farmer innovation and agricultural research* (Chambers, Pacey and Thrupp, 1989).

The *Farmer First* book argues that the approaches and methods of transfer of technology which have served industrial and green revolution agriculture, do not fit the resource-poor farming of the third, complex, diverse and risk-prone agriculture. It contrasts the more traditional, technology-driven agriculture, with its standardizing package of practices, with the complementary farmer-first approach or paradigm, which generates baskets of choices to enable farmers to vary, complicate and diversify their farming systems. It stresses, illustrates and explores the abilities of resource-poor farmers to experiment, adapt and innovate; the importance of giving priority to farmers' agendas and knowledge; a range of practical approaches and methods for farmer participation in research; and the implications for outsiders' roles and for institutions.

Since 1989, when *Farmer First* was published, much has happened. The analysis and thrust of that book have been more and more widely accepted. Growing numbers of professionals have made personal changes and accepted risks by advocating and adopting a farmer-first approach. But many scientists, teachers and extensionists are still trapped in top-down, centre-outwards institutions and transfer of technology (TOT) thinking and action, where 'we' determine priorities, generate technologies and then transfer them to farmers, and where farmers' participation is limited to adoption. All too easily, the farmer-first label and the rhetoric of participation have been adopted without the substance. A huge task remains for the personal, professional and institutional changes needed to enable research and extension adequately to serve resource-poor farm families. The changes advocated in the *Farmer First* book are still nowhere near being realized on the scale or with the commitment needed.

The arguments, cases and recommendations of that book stand, if anything with more force now in 1994 than they did in 1989. Increasingly, they apply not just to complex, diverse, risk-prone agriculture, but also to green revolution and industrial agriculture, especially as subsidies are reduced and farming systems are complicated, diversified and intensified. The number of very poor people in the world has also increased. Those whose livelihoods depend on the third agriculture have risen by some 100 to 200 million, to a total now of over 1.5 billion. Sustainable livelihoods with adequate food and decent incomes from complex, diverse, risk-prone agriculture become an ever-higher priority as pressures mount on the environment and on urban life and services through migration. So more than ever it is vital for professionals to struggle to learn how to serve vulnerable and resource-poor farmers better.

Fortunately, the frontiers of professional insights and methods have continued to be explored and opened up. As part of this, the Sustainable Agriculture Programme of the International Institute for Environment and Development conceived a three-year programme of research support and institutional collaboration entitled '*Beyond Farmer First: Rural People's Knowledge, Agricultural Research and Extension Practice*'. Collaborators in a dozen countries prepared detailed case studies on the interplay between formal and informal knowledge systems and assessed the wider implications for agricultural research and extension practice. The cases were presented and reviewed, along with a variety of discussion papers prepared by a diverse group of researchers on key theoretical, methodological and institutional issues surrounding knowledge, power and agricultural science, at the Institute of Development Studies, University of Sussex, in October 1992. Together, they provide the basis for this book.

Readers who have been trying to achieve farmer-first objectives may note some new language and critical comments. Both the language and the comments deserve to be taken seriously. Scientists and extensionists who have been struggling in the field to offset biases against women, the poor and the excluded can take heart that they have already moved away from what is described here as 'naive populism'. In a farmer-first mode, more and more people have become sensitive to social inequality and differences, gaining insights and developing practices parallel to those presented and advocated in this book.

It is, though, more than just the language that has changed and moved on. Sometimes new words say old things, but important new things are also being said. Even when some of the major points of *Beyond Farmer First* can be found in earlier work, they are new here in emphasis, elaboration and empirical evidence. Let me summarize how these new emphases appear to me. Three sets of insights stand out.

The first concerns power and the pluralism of knowledge. Systems of knowledge are many. Among these, modern science is only one, though the most powerful and universal. Rural people's knowledge is in contrast 'situated', differing both by locality and by group and individual, and differing in its modes of experimenting and learning: different people know different things in different places, and learn new things in different ways. These differences are reflected in and reinforce power and weakness. Scientific establishments and local elites (male, less poor, 'progressive') link together and monopolize some types of knowledge, while those who are weaker, dispersed and local are marginalized. The terms 'farmer', 'farm family', 'household' and 'community' need to be broken open, and differences of gender, age, social group and capability recognized and acted on.

Nor is knowledge just a stock, but a *process*. The issue is not just 'whose knowledge counts?', but 'who knows "who has access to what knowledge" and who can generate new knowledge, and how?' Especially, the questions are how those who are variously poor, weak, vulnerable, female and excluded can be strengthened in their own observations, experiments and analysis to generate and enhance their own knowledge; how they can better seek, demand, draw down, own and use information; how they can share and spread knowledge among themselves; and how they can influence formal agricultural research priorities.

The second set of insights concerns behaviour, interactions and methods. Farmers, extensionists and scientists are seen as social actors. Power relations are reflected in how they interact. The changes of role entailed in farmer-first approaches – for extensionists, to become not top-down TOT conveyor belts, but convenors, facilitators, catalysts, consultants and searchers and suppliers for farmers – these require changes in attitudes, behaviour and methods. The roles of farmers as observers, analysts, experimenters, monitors and evaluators require strengthening through new approaches and methods. Beyond the farmer-first repertoire of the late 1980s, there are now, as reported in this book, new methods and combinations of methods available, many involving visual analysis by groups. Poor people, whether literate or not, have in the early 1990s, in more than a score of countries, shown a far greater capacity to map, model, diagram, estimate, rank, score, experiment and analyse than outsider professionals have believed. Farmers have shown unexpected capabilities (even surprising themselves) and facilitators have a new and growing repertoire of analytical tools for farmers to use.

The third theme and set of insights concerns institutions. It is even clearer now than it was before that for organizations to facilitate participation requires that their own procedures, style and culture be participatory. Ways forward are presented by networks, alliances, lateral links, interactive learning environments and organizational strategies which permit and promote scaling up and spread. There are examples already and immense future opportunities in government departments, farmers' organizations and international organizations, as well as the more obvious and better documented NGOs. There are implications for authority, communications, personal attitudes and behaviour and relations between organizations. The changes required are reversals, from top-down hierarchies with supply-driven orders, targets and supervision, to bottom-up articulation of needs with demand-drawn search and supply, and lateral sharing.

Reversals imply a new professionalism. This is not a rejection of modem scientific knowledge, of research stations and laboratories, of scientific method. These remain potent, have their own validity and will always have their place. Rather it is a broadening, balancing and up-ending, to give a new primacy to the realities and analyses of poor people themselves. These themes and insights are liberating for agricultural scientists and extensionists, opening up new ranges of experience and ways of working. The comfortable certainties of known normal science are then complemented by the exciting unknowns which follow from facilitating analysis by poor rural people and learning from and with them. Anyone concerned with agricultural research and extension who reads this book can hardly fail to be thrown back to questions basic to the agricultural professions:

- Whose criteria and priorities count?
- Whose knowledge?
- Whose modes of learning and analysis?
- Whose tests, experiments, observations, assessments?
- Whose reality counts?

The logic and realism of this new professionalism deserve promotion now more than ever. Decentralization, diversity and empowerment of the poor become key values to focus effort. Direct and personal facilitation in the field, and learning from, with and by farmers, is invested with professional prestige.

The new professionalism is dynamic. Change accelerates. We, outsider professionals concerned with agricultural research and extension, and more broadly, with rural development, have always to ask: what should we now be doing? The contributions to this book point forward to new issues, new challenges and new opportunities. To address these issues, meet these challenges and seize these opportunities makes demands in different ways on all actors in agricultural policy, research and extension: to question, innovate, take risks, embrace errors, and learn; to create and support new environments for learning and enabling; to develop, adopt and spread new methods and approaches; to form new alliances and associations; to articulate a vision of a new agriculture of equity and participation; and in many ways, in many places, to work to make that vision real, with poor farmers gaining more say and playing more of a part in the processes of agricultural research and extension, the better to serve and sustain their lives and livelihoods.

Farmer First Revisited (2009)

The road travelled

In the 20 years since the Farmer First workshop, we have come a long way. That workshop, held at the Institute of Development Studies (IDS) in June 1987, followed five years of searching and finding people who were innovating with or writing about participatory approaches in agricultural research. They were marginalized in their organizations. Some felt they had to work in semi-secret and hide what they were doing from their colleagues. Meeting others similarly placed created a buzz of mutual recognition, reassurance, and excitement. We became what now we call a community of practice, with a hope of being part of a wave of the future.

Many of the original Farmer First concerns and insights seem still valid and useful: the three broad categories of types of agriculture (industrial, Green Revolution and the third agriculture that is CDR or complex, diverse and risk-prone); the recognition that the pipeline approaches and methods of transfer of technology (TOT) for the uniform and controlled conditions of industrial and green revolution agriculture did not fit CDR conditions; farmers' practices seen as adaptive performance; the proposition that adoption by farmers is validation of a technology; the comparative advantages of farmers over scientists in innovating for complex systems; and many others. Farmer First was established as paradigmatically different from TOT, and vital for CDR agriculture. It became a movement.

Five years later, in 1992, Ian Scoones and John Thompson convened a second workshop, Beyond Farmer First. This stressed perspectives that broadened and complemented Farmer First: the pluralism of different knowledges; the recognition of knowledge as not a stock but a process; seeing farmers, extensionists, scientists and others as social actors; recognizing political dimensions and the significance of power relations; and elements of a new professionalism in agricultural science.

As a workshop, Farmer First Revisited, held at IDS in December 2007, differed from the original Farmer First. Its organization and efficiency were a dramatic contrast. With Farmer First we had over 40 papers most of which were brought in hard copy by participants as they arrived. All three photocopiers broke down. Much of the conference was a self-organizing system on the edge of chaos, driven and saved by the excitement, energy, stamina and vision of individuals. And we had five days for it. With Farmer First Revisited almost all the papers were submitted and read by synthesizing presenters in advance. And we managed in only three days. The accomplished organization and facilitation by the IDS Knowledge, Technology and Society team showed how far we have come in learning how to prepare and manage such occasions.

But both were hugely exciting. In Farmer First it was mutual recognition of marginalized innovators, the solidarity of heretics, the sense of being a vanguard, of having a common commitment that could be transformative. In Farmer First Revisited it was seeing how far we had come, how many more domains than just farmer participation were relevant, and how rich the range of innovations had been. In Farmer First the focus was on the complexity and diversity of farming systems and the creativity of farmers. In Farmer First Revisited it was the complexity and diversity of domains of action and intervention and of relationships, and the co-creativity of many different actors.

Revisiting Farmer First, taking stock and looking forward now has been timely. As Ian Scoones and John Thompson summarize in their introduction to this book, much has changed; and agriculture, after a puzzling phase of neglect, is back again high on the development agenda. Food shortages, high food prices, and the focus on poverty reduction, make it ever more a priority. As a sort of Rip Van Winkle who, if not totally dormant, has been lurking and listening rather than engaging fully with agriculture during the past 20 years, two changes have struck me with force.

The first is the explosive proliferation of participatory methodologies, most of these involving and empowering farmers. These include: as before, farmers' research and participation in research; the many methodologies associated with the Participatory Research and Gender Analysis (PRGA) network of the CGIAR; farmer field schools and integrated pest management; the local agricultural research committees (CIALs) in Latin America; the involvement of farmers in all stages of seed breeding; the multiplicity of participatory approaches and practices in agricultural extension; participatory dimensions of the Institutional Learning and Change (ILAC) initiative in the CGIAR; and farmer participation in collaborative management, in market chains, in impact assessment and in policy processes. And these are not all. Many of these and others are represented in this book.

The second is how much realities, practices, vocabulary and concepts have changed and how these have changed in consonance together. Many of the words and expressions used and to be found in this book are either new or were little used in those earlier days. They expand the boundaries of what is seen as relevant. These boundaries have spread and become more inclusive, extending into and intensifying five domains that were earlier ignored or less recognized.

First, conceptually in 1987 our concern was to move beyond the reductionism of production and productivity and to privilege the complex, diverse and risk-prone realities of the majority of farmers, focusing on participation on-farm with and by farmers. Now it is the universe of concern itself that is complex and diverse. Many aspects are multiple or multi: we have, again and again, multiple stakeholders, multiple perspectives, multiple realities, multi-functional agriculture, multi-method approaches. Then too there are concepts and domains that are new or new in emphasis like food systems, food sovereignty, green trade, fair trade, market chains, value chains, innovation pathways and most of all innovation systems.

Second, formal organizations considered then were primarily those for agricultural research, extension and education. In addition, now we have farmers' organizations, farmers' movements, the private sector, marketing organizations, various forms of public–private collaboration and farmer participation in management.

Third, the relationships, interactions and processes on which we concentrated in Farmer First were between farmers and outsider professionals. Behaviour and attitudes were important. A key insight was Paul Richard's point that farming was an adaptive performance. Participatory approaches and processes were central. Now relationships and interactions are seen more clearly to have dimensions that are political and related to power, trust, transparency and accountability. Relationships are expressed in many forms. We have communities of practice and innovation alliances. Networks and partnerships have proliferated: networks are of many types – social, virtual, grassroots, peer and advice networks, and some sometimes are described as embedded or dense or unsupervised. So too with partnerships: we have public–private partnerships, multi-stakeholder partnerships, messy partnerships, partnerships for action research and others. And for many forms of collaboration we have 'co-' expressions – co-management, co-breeding, co-evolution, co-creation, co-development.

Fourth, pervasively, there is learning – action learning, learning alliances, learning laboratories, experiential learning, alternative learning, interactive learning, policy learning, collective learning, discovery learning, shared learning and change, and recognition that many organizations have cultures that can be described as non-learning.

Finally, on the personal side, there is now concern not just with capacity building or capacity development, but with mindsets, soft skills, and the language of reflexivity and values.

Language, perceptions, priorities and realities interact. Some language is window-dressing and cosmetic. But these five domains and activities and the language that goes with them represent real change, bringing with them complexity and a higher priority to relationships. All this is manifest, again and again, in this book. And its evidence, analysis and synthesis together provide a foundation, platform and launching pad for future innovation and practice.

Challenges now: to make a difference

Many of the challenges are still those of 20 years ago. The paradigm of pipeline research and transfer of technology, of top-down packages of practices passed on to farmers, of the demand for an Indian-style Green Revolution in Africa, of big and quick fixes, is embedded in mindsets and bureaucratic imperatives. It is resilient and keeps reasserting itself. In prescriptions and programmes for African agriculture that come from outside Africa the transfer of technology model has been not only alive and well but flourishing. In the early years, the mechanistic Training and Visit (T&V) system persisted, at least in Africa, provoking the verse:

> If Asian countries throw it out
> It's only they who have the clout
> In Africa you can insist
> They have no power to resist

Even in Africa, though, T&V was eventually buried, though for a time replaced by the activities of the early Sasakawa Global 2000 programme. The failure to understand the difference between the Green Revolution of north-west India, with its flat and uniform land, reliable irrigation, low rainfall, and good access to inputs and markets, and in contrast most of the agriculture of Sub-Saharan Africa, with its undulating, diverse, unirrigated land and often with poor access, reflects a failure of agricultural education and of policy-makers' perceptions. There has been an inappropriate transfer of mindsets.

The Farmer First Revisited workshop and this book show that we are in another space, more extensive, more complex and more diverse, paradigmatically embracing Farmer First but going far beyond it. If a focus of Farmer First was farmers' potential and performance, and of Beyond Farmer First process and power, the core focus of Farmer First Revisited is people and professionalism. The new demands, emphases and activities point more than ever to the priorities of personal and professional reflexivity, to changing roles and to methodologies.

Reflexivity refers to self-critical self-awareness of one's mindset, mental frames, predispositions, perceptions, and orientations, including values, and what constitutes rigour and valid evidence. At the end of their introduction to this book, the editors point to the need for 'fundamental shifts in thinking in practice', and for innovation systems which normatively engage with issues of 'power, politics, learning and reflexivity'. These have emerged from the Farmer First Revisited process as frontiers now for intense attention.

Roles are now wider, either new or new in emphasis. Farmers, as envisaged in Farmer First, were seen as innovators, as peers who can share experiences, and as experts who could inform scientists; these they remain, but in Farmer First Revisited they also have roles in advocacy, politics, and marketing. Farmers are recognized as social analysts, organizers, activists and politicians. The roles for scientists, extensionists and other non-farming professionals are too being defined more widely and differently: not just as champions or innovators, but as technology intermediaries, translators, brokers, negotiators, and facilitators, all of these demanding orientations and aptitudes beyond their traditional roles.

To support reflexivity and new roles requires new methodologies. These can be high-yielding by extending like other Farmer First Revisited concerns into far more domains than those of Farmer First. The opportunity is to develop methodologies and then enable them to spread, evolving and improving as they go. To illustrate, they might include how to:

- Facilitate collective and individual reflection on mindsets and biases, and move and transform these from transfer of technology and pipeline to people-centred innovation and learning.
- Train in facilitation so that facilitation becomes embedded as a way of interacting and relating with others, as already begun by the Institutional Learning and Change (ILAC) initiative in the CGIAR.
- Brainstorm to identify, explore and move towards centre stage, those domains (high-yielding gaps) whose neglect suggests large unexploited potentials (for example, rooting systems, soil biota and high-yielding principles such as sensitive nurturing of individual plants in conditions that allow the full expression of their potentials, as with the System of Rice Intensification).

- Develop and introduce new curricula, approaches and methods, attitudes, behaviours and relationships of participatory teaching and learning, into agricultural education and training.
- Sustain innovation and synergies of change over years by bringing together scientists, academic teachers, extensionists and farmers for experiential learning, transforming relationships and evolving and establishing new norms of professionalism.

Readers will find more methodologies to add from this book. The challenge is to recognize the importance of methodological innovation and put it more on the map. It is to learn how better to identify points of entry and high leverage, and processes and times and places when small pushes can move whole systems into better pathways. If the Farmer First workshop helped to provoke, inspire and support the explosion of participatory research with and by farmers, can and will Farmer First Revisited help to provoke, inspire and support another rich proliferation of methodologies, but now across a wider range, and their spread and continuing evolution?

So what?

The implications of the many ideas and experiences in this book resonate with, but go beyond, reflexivity, roles and methodologies. For all of these point to the personal dimension, so central and yet so habitually neglected.

What sort of people we are and what we do is fundamental to good practice for all professionals involved with agriculture. And like pro-poor agricultural development, people too are complex and diverse and have multiple dimensions, emotional as well as mental. Participants in the workshop who spoke about this saw no contradiction between head and heart. Heart fuels the fire and commitment that energize head. Anger, passion and enthusiasm were recognized as drivers to be combined with vision and courage; and it is these together that make champions of change.

The test of a workshop and of a book is what difference they make. Ian Scoones and John Thompson have been masterly in ordering, analysing and presenting material that is more complex and diverse, and which covers a far wider range of relevance, than confronted the editors of *Farmer First*. They have managed to make this a resource to bring the reader accessibly up-to-date in a field which has become wider and harder to grasp. The questions now are: Who will read and act on the evidence, insights and conclusions of this book? Who will become the reflexive and committed new professionals? Research scientists and their managers? University faculty and those who design curricula? Fieldworkers in agricultural extension? Front-line staff in NGOs, marketing organizations and the private sector and those who manage them? Government officials, political leaders, staff of funding agencies, policy-makers and influencers who sit on committees? And not least, and increasingly, farmers themselves? It is all of them who can make a difference. It is for all of them that this book is written.

In 20 years' time, if there is another Farmer First workshop, will they say of the latter 2000s: 'By then, they could see the problems and opportunities, and the directions needed for change. The elements of the new professionalism were clear: they are there in the book'? And as they look back, will they then ask:

- 'Why was agricultural education not transformed?
- Why did agricultural bureaucracies remain so top-down?
- Why did so much agricultural research remain upstream?
- Why did resource-poor farmers continue to be marginal?
- Why was the cornucopia of promising innovations never taken to scale? And, above all
- Why were behaviour, attitudes and personal reflexivity never put at the core of professionalism?'

Or will they look back and see the latter 2000s as a turning point, with this book playing a part? Will they struggle to imagine themselves trapped in the mindsets, methods, misunderstandings and misprescriptions that had earlier prevailed? Will they see the time of the workshop and of this book as a tipping point, a watershed?

Neither is likely in full. What happens next will depend not least on getting to grips with power, politics, relationships, and reflexivity. These have not been traditional concerns of most funders or of those professionally engaged with agriculture. They are outside their normal interests and comfort zones. Yet they are crucial for the transformations needed now. We must find new ways to engage in constructive dialogue around these themes, and to map new directions for agricultural research, education and development.

This book reviews much of the state of the art, is grounded in experience, and provides signposts to the future. The editors and authors are on the frontiers of exploration and innovation. They give a head start for the next stages of the journey. Progress now depends on personal and collective vision and commitment. May many be encouraged by what is presented here and supported and inspired to become pioneers and champions of transformative change.

Source: Scoones, I. and Thompson, J. (2009) *Farmer first revisited*. Rugby: Practical Action Publishing. ISBN 978 1 85339 682 3. http://doi.org/10.3362/9781780440149

Source: Scoones, I. and Thompson, J. (1994) *Beyond farmer first*. Rugby: Practical Action Publishing. http://doi.org/10.3362/9781780442372

Reflections from John Thompson

John Thompson is a resource geographer and Research Fellow at the Institute of Development Studies (IDS), UK, with a 35-year record of academic and applied research on the socio-technical and political economic dimensions of agrarian change and rural transformation in sub-Saharan Africa, Latin America, South and Southeast Asia, UK, and USA. He serves as Director of the Future Agricultural Consortium, a network of African and international researchers which conducts comparative, mixed-methods research on agricultural policy processes in Africa and as Deputy Director of the Sussex Sustainability Research Programme, which analyses synergies and trade-offs among the UN Sustainable Development Goals.

Looking back to look 'foreword': Reflections on changing views and approaches to putting farmers first in agricultural research and development practice

The three books entitled *Farmer First* (Chambers et al. 1989), *Beyond Farmer First* (Scoones and Thompson 1994), and *Farmer First Revisited* (Scoones and Thompson 2009) drew on over 20 years of critical reflection and detailed empirical observation and experimentation on incorporating farmer knowledge and innovation in agricultural research and development practice. Between them, they elaborated the philosophical and methodological underpinnings of what has come to be known as the 'Farmer First approach', informed by three international workshops and the contributions of well over 100 scholars and practitioners from around the world.

Collectively, these authors sought to challenge the top-down and linear narratives, models, and practices that came to dominate much agricultural research and development in the late 20th and early 21st centuries. These tended to prioritize external technologies and expert knowledge over local knowledge and practices and to undervalue the agency and innovation of farmers and other rural people. In contrast, the Farmer First approach prioritized participatory methods and practices that empowered farmers to co-design and co-implement research and development interventions that were farmer-led and context-specific.

When the third of the Farmer First volumes was published in 2009, my co-editor Ian Scoones and I invited Robert to write the foreword for it (as he had done for the previous two books). He used the opportunity to look to the future and anticipate how international agricultural research and development would evolve, highlighting both the potential innovations and the likely unresolved challenges, writing (Chambers 2009: xxiv–xxv):

> *In 20 years' time, if there is another Farmer First workshop, will they say of the latter 2000s: 'By then, they could see the problems and opportunities, and the directions needed for change?' ... Or will they look back and see [this period] as a turning point...? Will they struggle to imagine themselves trapped in the mindsets, methods, misunderstandings and misprescriptions that had earlier prevailed? Will they see the time of... this workshop and this book as a tipping point, a watershed? ... Neither is likely in full. What happens next will depend not least on getting to grips with power, politics, relationships and reflexivity. These have not been traditional concerns of most funders or of those professionally engaged with agriculture. They are outside their normal interests and comfort zones. Yet they are crucial for the transformations needed now. We must find new ways to engage in constructive dialogue around these themes, and to map new directions for agricultural research, education and development.*

From the current vantage point, roughly 15 years since that writing, we can see how prescient Robert's words were. A great deal has changed over this period. New shocks and stresses are evident – from climate change to the Covid-19 pandemic – with major implications for farming livelihoods and agricultural research and development. New economic relations and connections are apparent, particularly around the market, with increasingly globalized linkages. New patterns of urbanization and industrialization are affecting the roles of agriculture in wider economic and political processes. And new agricultural technologies, including genetically modified and 'climate smart' crops, offer both opportunities and risks. Access to those technologies is an increasing concern, as patterns of ownership shift towards the private sector and public provision continues to decline. Consequently, complex, uncertain, multi-scaled processes and interactions in agricultural systems are emerging from the intertwining of social, technological, and ecological dynamics in different settings. These, in turn, are leading to the emergence of and trade-offs between different pathways to more sustainable systems, and a growing recognition of the importance of surprise and adaptive response in agricultural policy and related research and development processes.

Yet much remains the same – particularly in the poorer, marginalized parts of the world: the complex, diverse, and risk-prone environments where

Farmer First approaches were first advocated. Agriculture remains the main source of livelihoods for a significant proportion of rural people in those places, and for many countries, it is a key driver of sustained, employment-based growth.

Against this backdrop, the agricultural research and development community continues to struggle with narrow mindsets, restricted methods, rigid organizational structures, and multiple misunderstandings and misprescriptions about the capabilities and livelihood aspirations of rural people. This reinforces dominant patterns of knowledge creation and application, exacerbates patterns of inequity and exclusion, and pursues 'silver bullet' techno-fixes to complex problems that require more nuanced, gender-sensitive, and context-specific solutions. Unfortunately, large national and international research and development organizations only rarely recognize how radically they need to change their procedures, incentives, and relationships if they are to practise and promote participation in more than just name.

The good news is that much has been learned about bad practice in this intervening period, especially about going to scale too fast and the contradictions between participation and top-down drivers and demands. A great deal has also been learned about embedded obstacles to participation, notably in institutional cultures and practices and in individual mindsets, values, attitudes, and behaviours. Seeing how these interlock helps clarify what needs to change.

In recent years, the Farmer First approach has evolved to include a recognition of the complexity of not only agricultural systems, but food systems more broadly. This Food Systems approach builds on the principles of Farmer First, emphasizing the importance of inclusive and participatory processes and collaboration between farmers and others. However, it also expands the scope of inquiry to include higher-level issues such as policy processes, governance arrangements, and power relations, and it seeks to address systemic issues that cannot be solved by local-level, farmer-centred innovations alone. This approach recognizes the interconnectedness of different parts of the food system, from 'field to fork', and the need for coordinated action to address issues such as food and nutrition security, sustainability, and equity and social justice. This means embracing a diversity of perspectives and approaches, acknowledging trade-offs and tensions between them, and engaging with a host of different actors, each with their own interests and agendas. It also means recognizing the political economy of those systems and how this is both changing and changed by the way food is produced, transformed, consumed, and researched across the planet (Thompson and Sumberg 2012). In that sense, the core themes and central messages of the three Farmer First volumes, and Robert's forewords to them, remain as valid as ever.

References

Chambers, R. (2009). Foreword. In I. Scoones and J. Thompson (eds.), *Farmer First Revisited: Innovation for agricultural research and development*. Rugby: Practical Action Publishing, pp. xxiv–xxv.

Chambers, R., Pacey, A., and Thrupp, L-A. (eds.) (1989). *Farmer First: Farmer innovation and agricultural research*. London: Intermediate Technology Publications.

Scoones, I. and Thompson, J. (eds.) (1994). *Beyond Farmer First: Rural people's knowledge, agricultural research and extension practice*. London: Intermediate Technology Publications.

Scoones, I. and Thompson, J. (eds.) (2009). *Farmer First Revisited: Innovation for agricultural research and development*. Rugby: Practical Action Publishing.

Thompson, J. and Sumberg, J. (2012). *Nullius in verba*: Contestation, pathways and political agronomy. In J. Sumberg and J. Thompson (eds.), *Contested Agronomy: Agricultural Research in a Changing World*. London: Routledge, pp. 204–11.

Foreword to *South African Participatory Poverty Assessment* (1997)

> The use of Participatory Poverty Assessments (PPAs) grew significantly in the 1990s (Robb, 1998). They were a set of participatory methods designed to deepen the understanding of both the causes and the experience of poverty from the perspective of poor people themselves, and to communicate this understanding to decision makers in government and development agencies. Not surprisingly, Robert was a huge champion of this approach. South Africa's first, post-Independence PPA was conducted in 1997, and Robert was asked to write the foreword for the final report.

It is an honour to have been invited to write this foreword to the South African Participatory Poverty Assessment. This is not least because it has broken new ground in methods, process, presentation and findings, and because it has the potential to make so much difference for the better.

The most creative evolution of PPAs has been in Africa. Among these, the South African PPA has been unique in its design and process. Alone among PPAs in the world, it facilitated NGOs and researchers to undertake participatory studies in areas where they were already working, and on aspects of deprivation with which they were familiar. Alone among PPAs in the world, it had a transparency of process which was both courageous and outstandingly effective in difficult conditions. It was also unusual in the degree of ethical commitment to follow up with action in the communities which collaborated and gave their time and analysis to the study. The methods used to present and analyse findings were, to the best of my knowledge, new, with care taken not to impose outsiders' professional concepts and categories, but to allow the voices and experiences of poor people to present and construct their own realities. Those who conduct further PPAs, wherever in the world, would do well to study the approach and methods used here, and learn from these South African innovations.

Like its predecessors in Ghana and Zambia, many in the South African PPA used the powerful and popular approaches and methods of PRA (Participatory Rural Appraisal). These "hand over the stick" to local people to conduct their own analysis. Teams were trained, and then applied PRA. They empowered those who were weak, vulnerable, poor and marginalised to express and analyse their experience of deprivation, their problems, priorities and hopes. It is their voices that speak through these pages.

So it is that the findings stand out with sharp immediacy: the often unperceived seasonality of deprivation, even for those receiving pensions; time poverty – the poverty of lack of time among women; the crisis of wellbeing for children; the agony and frustration of trying to obtain justice from an indifferent or hostile administration; the lack of information – "We don't know what we can ask for, we don't know who to ask, and we don't know how to ask"; the isolation and suffering of women with children, deserted by men. The report is loud with the voices of the unheard. Let me not try to summarise. Let them speak for themselves, as they do with such eloquence.

The true test of a PPA is, though, not its methods or process, not its presentation, not its insights, but what difference it makes in practice. Good reports that lead to no change are bad reports. Up to this point, the South African PPA has been outstanding. There has also been commitment at the highest political level to action and follow through. The question is whether that can be sustained and expressed through the detail of changes in laws, administrative orders and procedures, through the allocation of resources, and above all through transforming the behaviour and attitudes of those with legal and administrative power at all levels.

Many of us from other parts of the world have come to look to South Africa for innovation and inspiration, and for showing that good things that seemed impossible can indeed be done. Leadership and example have come in full measure from the painful but peaceful processes of reconciliation, and the demonstration of the healing power of magnanimity and forgiveness. Now it has come too from the open and original processes of this PPA and the insights it has generated, giving voice to those who are marginal and excluded – single mothers, pensioners, old people, children, and others. The great question now is whether what has been expressed in these pages, what is now known, will lead to change, not just to policy-in-principle, but to policy in practice, to what happens on the ground, to what touches people and their lives.

This will depend on the sustained concern and commitment of political leaders, officials, and many other citizens. If South Africa can muster and maintain that concern and commitment, it will once again be a beacon to the rest of humankind. To the voices of the millions in South Africa and elsewhere whose lives could be transformed by the processes flowing from this PPA, let me add this hope: that those with power, at every level, will seize this great opportunity for deep and lasting changes for the better. If they do, the voices will not have been raised in vain, and the good outcomes will spread, not only in South Africa, but in the rest of the world.

26 June 1997 Robert Chambers

Source: May, J. 1998. *Experience and Perceptions of Poverty in South Africa: Final report*. Durban: Praxis Publishing. ISBN 0-620-22-763-X

Reflections from Keetie Roelen

> *Keetie Roelen is Senior Research Fellow and Co-Deputy Director of the Centre for the Study of Global Development at the Open University, UK. Her research focuses on areas of poverty, social protection, and anti-poverty interventions in relation to children, women, and psychosocial wellbeing. She is a mixed-methods researcher, holding both quantitative and qualitative research skills. She first learned about Robert's influential work more than two decades ago, as part of a team undertaking a participatory poverty assessment in northern Namibia, before working alongside him at IDS for 12 years.*

The beauty of life is that it is continuously shaped and reshaped by the footprints left by others. Some leave a small mark, others leave life-long imprints. For me, the latter is certainly the case with respect to Robert and his ground-breaking work on participatory poverty assessment (PPA).

My first encounter with PPA was two decades ago, in Namibia in 2003. Fresh out of university, I started an internship with the poverty unit at the United Nations Development Programme (UNDP). Having been a diligent student of the theory of development economics, it was exciting to be immersed in the practice of multilateral engagement on poverty reduction.

But once I found myself sitting at my desk in a shiny office on Windhoek's Independence Avenue, I felt far removed from the lived realities of people experiencing poverty. Much of the work struck me as abstract and top-down, with lots of talk about what constituted poverty and how to tackle it yet little engagement with those experiencing it. That is, until I was able to join the research team undertaking Namibia's first PPA.

I recall the 12-hour drive up north to Ohangwena region, during which my fellow passengers were excitedly discussing the tools they were going to use in the PPA exercise. A team member sitting next to me asked whether I had done any PPA work before. Feeling rather embarrassed, I had to admit that not only did I not have any experience, but I also hadn't even heard of PPA prior to coming to Namibia. My colleague raised an eyebrow and then rolled her eyes, probably wondering why I was taking up valuable space in the car. Meanwhile I was questioning the relevance of my economics degree.

I soon found out why the team was so enthusiastic. After having set up camp, we spent a week engaging with community members about their lives in the remote village of Etsapa. Walking from *kraal* to *kraal*, mapping the lay of the land, drawing daily activity clocks and debating wealth categories – it all provided immensely rich insight into residents' daily lives and how they experienced it. Concerns were raised about the poor state of roads leading into Etsapa, meaning villagers were virtually cut off from the outside world during periods of heavy rain. Frustration levels about the authorities' lack of action to improve access to schools and health clinics ran high.

I was enthralled. Bearing witness to lively discussions, sketching out seasonal calendars in the sand, using stones to rank the most important daily expenses – it all felt like a far cry from the economic models through which I had learned to understand the world. Simplistic assumptions about humans' rational behaviour suddenly seemed nonsensical. People and their lives are complex, underpinned by an intricate web of values, relationships, and strategies that we can only aim to understand by 'handing over the stick'.

It came as no surprise to find years later, when I joined IDS, that Robert Chambers was one of its most revered members of staff. My introduction to PPA was one of the most formative experiences in my life, and I quickly learned that I certainly wasn't the only one on whom Robert's work left a lasting mark.

In his foreword to the South African PPA, Robert notes that the true test of the PPA is the difference it makes in practice. When subjecting Robert's own work to this test, there is no doubt about its immense impact. Not only has he demonstrated the value of including and listening to the voices of those with lived experience, he has also equipped students, practitioners, and policy-makers alike with invaluable tools to put theory into practice and create lasting change.

Reference

Robb, C. 1998. *Can the Poor Influence Policy: Participatory poverty assessments in the developing world.* Washington, DC: World Bank.

Foreword to the Japanese translation (2000) of *Whose Reality Counts? Putting the first last* (1997)

> *Robert's central argument in this (hugely influential) book is that the development world has paid far too much attention to the views and ideas of those in power, and not nearly enough to those who are not. As a result, numerous mistakes have been made.* Whose Reality Counts *is a sequel to his earlier book,* Rural Development: Putting the last first *(1983). It is designed also as a guide to existing and emerging participatory methodologies that allow for different ways of doing and knowing. His foreword in the Japanese translation of the book is interesting because it was written three years after the publication of the original text.*

In the few years since this book was written dramatic changes have continued in the field of development. Old and new certainties have continued to be challenged. The development model of the East Asian tigers has imploded. The scale of human deprivation has not diminished, and the gaps between poor and rich, between underclass and overclass, have continued to widen. Emphases and priorities have shifted. Good governance, attacking corruption, and capacity building have rapidly come to be seen as keys to other good change. Meanwhile, globalisation, like a virus, benign or otherwise, has extended to more and more domains. And sadly there is much more to add to any list of errors of judgement and action in development policy and practice.

In parallel, the rhetoric of participation has spread exponentially to the point at which it is now normal, and to be expected. But practice lags far behind words, and good practice lags behind bad practice. The directions of change are, though, encouraging. Those big people who make speeches, and even perhaps those less big people who write them, increasingly recognise that participation cannot be commanded, that good practice cannot be assumed, that going to scale with participation means trading off quality against quantity, that participatory approaches require and generate professional, institutional, and personal change. We are moving into new spaces, into uncharted seas. We have compasses in individual conscience and commitment but maps we do not have; and the tides, currents and waves seem ever harder to predict.

These conditions reinforce the main messages of this book. If "we", who are not poor, are serious about reducing poverty, it is more than ever "we" who have to change. If Governments and NGOs are to be effective, they have, more than ever, to become less hierarchical and less centralised, and their policies and practices less standardised, and more flexible, adaptive and diverse. If universities and training institutes are to do less damage and more good, they have, more than ever, to shift from didactic to empowering and participatory ways of enabling students and trainees to learn. If poor people are truly to improve their experience of life, shifting from a bad to a good experience of life, whole systems of government, civil society and private sector organisations have to change their procedures, values and cultures. The opportunity, need and imperative are, more than ever, for "uppers" to gain fulfilment from disempowering themselves, and empowering "lowers".

In most fields now, there are signs of changes in these directions. It is perhaps least noticeable among multi-national corporations. It is perhaps most evident among younger people working in development, and in some NGOs and donor agencies. Some Governments and parts of Governments in developing countries are also, to an impressive degree, struggling to internalise the values, behaviours and attitudes of participation. Governments and their staff, in countries as diverse as Bolivia, Ghana, India, Tanzania, Uganda and Vietnam, have increasingly become engaged with participatory approaches. Participatory Poverty Assessments (PPAs) have continued to spread and to evolve ethical and effective procedures. The Uganda Participatory Poverty Appraisal Process is a beacon of hope, for it has already led to pro-poor policy change. Owned by the Uganda Government, based in the Ministry of Finance, and respected by donors for the quality of its work, it presents an example to the rest of the world, including the rich countries of the North, showing what can be achieved through good participation with political support.

I feel that in this foreword I ought to be pointing to errors in the book, and revisions that I would now like to make. I am slightly ashamed to say that, despite the rapid changes that continue to take place, there is little I would wish to change. There are only things that I would add.

For example, there have been developments with participatory methodologies, and with PRA in particular. PRA has spread increasingly to countries in the North. Participatory monitoring and evaluation is emerging as the linchpin of sustainable change to participatory modes of interaction. Sharing, as one of the pillars of PRA, is being strengthened with the word partnership to become "sharing and partnership". Pluralistic sharing between methodologies with different labels has become the norm. For its part, PRA, having started life as Participatory Rural Appraisal, is now sometimes taken as Participatory Reflection and Action. For the personal dimension, and self-critical reflection, have continued to be seen as more and more central to good practice. As participation becomes higher profile, so critics increasingly are willing to contribute to understanding and practice. Unfortunately, those that stand outside and have not experienced the responsibilities, ethical dilemmas, problems and fulfilments of practitioners are often wide of the mark. Practitioners themselves, in their autocritiques, remain the most perceptive, and those from whom there is most to learn.

So asking "Whose Reality Counts?" seems, if anything, even more crucial now, at the start of the third millennium, than it was a few years ago when the book was written. This makes me especially delighted to introduce this Japanese edition. There is no way I can thank enough those who, through their commitment and painstaking efforts, have translated this book. Naoto Noda has been the prime mover, sharing overall responsibility with Kiyoshi Shiratori. With their leadership and coordination, the translation has been an extraordinarily participatory affair, carried out with no less than 14 others: Nobuhiro Haraikawa, Chie Sato, Hiromi Iseki, Tsuyoshi Ito, Ayumu Oshima, Ritsuko Hagiwara, Yumiko Nishimura, Masato Noda, Hideo Toyota, Mao Okuda, Mio Takada, Hiroto Mitsugi, Hana Kobayashi, and Keiko Kani. All of those named, and their families, will have made many sacrifices to bring this work to completion. I hope that readers will join me in thanking them most profoundly for this translation.

Let me hope, too, that those who read it will find here a challenge to rethink which leads to action. But beware! I have sometimes inscribed the book with these words:

Health Warning!
Read at your own risk
The author accepts no responsibility
For damage to the career of
Any person reading this book

This is half joke, half serious. For the challenge is to stand on one's head, to see things differently, to think differently, and to act differently; and these are not always easy or popular. Some who have tried have been not promoted but dismissed, even in NGOs. But cultures and practices are changing. The warning may already be out of date. It is up to all of us to make it so, to make it safe for others to join the vanguard.

3 October 1999   Robert Chambers

Source: Japanese translation (1999, Tokyo: Akashi Shoten) of Chambers, R. (1997) *Whose Reality Counts? Putting the first last*. Rugby: Practical Action Publishing

Reflections from Rosemary McGee

> Rosie McGee is an interdisciplinary development studies professional with a background in NGO advocacy and over 20 years as a Research Fellow at IDS. Strongly influenced by Robert Chambers in her PhD research and policy advocacy work, she was recruited into IDS's Participation Group by him in 1999. A longstanding member of the teaching team on IDS's MA in Power, Participation and Social Change, which Robert helped design and launch in 2004, Rosie's research focuses on understanding and shifting power relations in development and social change work, currently in relation to just energy transitions, and to gender backlash.

I bought *Whose Reality Counts? Putting the first last* in Manchester in August 1997, as soon as I returned from a year of PhD fieldwork the purpose and design of which were strongly influenced by Robert's key ideas of the previous 15 years. During my year of ethnographic fieldwork in a remote rural community at the end of the road in a guerrilla-controlled area high in the western cordillera of the Colombian Andes, I had translated the precursor working paper 'Poverty and livelihoods: Whose reality counts?' into Spanish. It was a desperate attempt to get its ideas – later unpacked in more depth in *Whose Reality Counts?* – into the hands and minds of Colombian development decision makers, practitioners, and scholars.

My PhD explored the notion of a 'perception gap' between policy-makers' and poor people's views on the issue of poverty and how it may be reduced. In the community where I lived and conducted fieldwork from 1996 to 1997, the confining category of income poverty flew in the face of the complex, multidimensional livelihood ailments and crises that every single inhabitant navigated every day. People's access to basic public services was determined by a blunt and blinkered survey questionnaire so distorting that it led to the community's self-evidently wealthiest inhabitants getting cheaper access to services than the self-evidently poorest. How could National Planning Department researchers and policy-makers fail to see that their World Bank-based definition of poverty and their survey questionnaire-based targeting system, the gatekeeper to crucial public service subsidies, distorted rural and poor urban realities to the point of nonsense, and institutionalized inequity and clientelism in social protection targeting? Could they *want* it to compound the marginality of the marginalized?

My path since has reflected the proposals set out in *Whose Reality Counts?* My first post-PhD job was to promote participatory and gender-aware approaches in an international development NGO's policy, advocacy, partnerships, and operational work. From 1998 to 2000 I worked on the Uganda Participatory Poverty Assessment (1998–2002), confirming what I'd learned from fieldwork and from Robert about how rich and complex the life worlds of marginalized people were and deepening my conviction that usually poor and marginalized people remain 'last' not because of any lack of knowledge about their situations or how these could be improved, but because of the interests of the 'first'.

In 1999 I joined the Participation Group at IDS and since then have sought to challenge empty and co-opted participation rhetoric, understand how power works, bring the realities of practice and of marginality closer to the sanitized central zones where decisions are made to try to shift incentives and interests, and facilitate development and change practitioners to know and see differently.

There remains little that needs changing in the key messages of *Whose Reality Counts? Putting the first last*. Since its publication, socioeconomic and cultural inequality has deepened; consumerist capitalism has permeated and vitiated value systems; the climate has changed to a point that is very nearly irreversible; the foundations of democratic politics and within it gender, racial, and epistemic justice are being systematically rolled back. Robert was simply a few decades ahead of most of us in formulating these messages, which will take so long to enact. Re-reading him now is a way to overcome fatigue and re-vitalize struggles.

Foreword to *The Myth of Community: Gender issues in participatory development* (1998) by Irene Guijt and Meera Kaul Shah

> As commented on by Robert in his foreword, this was the first book that brought together gender and participation. The authors set out to critically reflect on both the understanding of gender within participatory development, and the use of participatory methods within gender-based development work. It grew out of a two-day workshop that the editors convened at IDS in 1993. Robert's foreword text here is followed by a reflection from Andrea Cornwall, one of the original contributing authors to The Myth of Community.

The Myth of Community fills a huge gap. With hindsight, the previous lack of a book like this appears little short of spectacular. During the past two decades, the two powerful but separate movements, of gender and of participation, have been transforming the rhetoric, and increasingly the reality, of local-level development. Each has generated much writing. Each has major implications for the other. Yet, astonishingly, to the best of my knowledge, this is the first book thoroughly to explore the overlaps, linkages, contradictions, and synergies between the two. It cannot be often that a vital gap cries out for so long to be filled; and that it is then filled so well, with such rich material and insight, and with so much of the excitement of significant discovery, as in this book.

Its importance can be understood against the background of the two movements.

First, gender and development has had an immense influence. In many ways – in rhetoric and syntax, in appointments and promotions, in organizational behaviour, in projects, programmes and policies, and above all in personal awareness and orientation – a tidal change has started and continues. At the personal level, many of us development professionals have been both threatened and liberated as we become more aware of the pervasive inequities of the socially constructed relations between women and men and recognize the personal implications for ourselves. To be sure, there is far still to go; and whether we are women or men, we will always have much to learn and unlearn, and much to work to change. But in development thinking and action, the direction is clear. Gender awareness and equity are irreversibly on the agenda and increasingly pursued in practice.

For its part, participation has origins which go far back. It has, though, only recently come together in the mainstream of development discourse and action. Both donor agencies and governments now have policies to promote it. At the same time, methodologies for participatory development, among them PRA (originally participatory rural appraisal), have evolved and spread, presenting new opportunities and means for turning the rhetoric into reality. Participation, like gender, presents challenges and opportunities across a wide front. Not least these are institutional, to change organizations, and personal, to change individual behaviour and attitudes.

To explore and share experiences and ideas about gender and participation, Irene Guijt and Meera Shah convened a two-day workshop at the Institute of Development Studies (IDS) at the University of Sussex, UK in December 1993. It was one of a series on PRA organized jointly by IDS and the International Institute for Environment and Development, London. This book originates in the discussions and papers of that workshop. Papers have been updated and revised; others have been added; and the scope has been widened beyond PRA to include participatory approaches more broadly.

There is here a rich and diverse harvest for the reader. Across the board, the contributions offer insights. The direct personal experiences of the writers present an immediacy and realism which carries conviction. The realities described invite reflection. They provoke review and revision of one's sense of what is right and what is doable. Each reader will draw out her or his own themes and lessons. For me, four stand out.

First, there are many *biases* to be recognized and offset. Attitudes and behaviours which are dominating and discriminatory are common among those of us who are men: to become aware of these is a first and often difficult step. Even when the application of participatory methodologies is intended to minimize biases, women are often marginalized. Again and again, women are excluded by factors like time and place of meeting, composition of groups, conventions that only men speak in public, outsiders being only or mainly men, and men talking to men. In communities, it is easier for men than women to find the undisturbed blocks of time needed for PRA mapping, diagramming, discussions and analysis. The times best for women to meet, sometimes late after dark, are often inconvenient for outsiders. When outsiders rush, make short visits, do not stay the night, and come only once or twice, it is typically difficult for local women to participate, and issues of gender are likely to be marginalized or excluded. Again and again, the cases cited in this book are, in contrast, based on repeated, sustained and sensitive contact and interaction. Recognizing and offsetting these biases requires sensitivity, patience and commitment on the part of those who are outsiders to a community.

Second, local *contexts* are complex, diverse and dynamic. The reductionism of collective nouns misleads: 'community' hides many divisions and differences, with gender often hugely significant; 'women' as a focus distracts attention from gender relations between women and men, and from men themselves; and 'women' also conceals the many differences between females by age, class, marital status and social group. Nor are common beliefs valid everywhere: female-headed households are often the worst off, but not always. Moreover, social relations change, sometimes fast. It is not just the myth of community that this book dispels, but other myths of simple, stable and uniform social realities.

Third, *conflict* is sometimes necessary and positive for good change. For gender equity, much that needs to change concerns the power and priority of males over females. Several contributions to this book strikingly confront consensual participation as a myth, at least in the short term. They show that conflict can be an essential and creative factor in change for the better. Common examples are tackling issues of power and control over resources and dealing with aggressive and violent behaviour. Domestic violence, drunken husbands, female infanticide, discrimination against females of all ages – these are phenomena difficult to confront without conflict. This does not mean a negative sum in well-being, that for females to gain, males must lose. To cease to dominate, oppress or be violent is itself a liberation. Responsible well-being is enhanced in shared responsibilities, in good relations in the family, in social harmony, and in personal peace of mind. The key is to facilitate changes in gender relations which lead to a positive sum, in which all come to feel better off, and so in which all gain.

Fourth, issues of *ethics* are repeatedly posed by both gender and participation: whether outsiders' interventions are based on universally valid values or a form of cultural domination; whether working with those who are weak and vulnerable leads to bad results for them, as when women are beaten by their husbands when the outsider leaves; whether gender-sensitive participation leads in practice to women and girls being better off or through a backlash worse off than before. There seem to be no easy answers. The imperative is to consult women and girls, and sometimes men, and seek their views on what it is right and practicable to do; it is to recognize the dilemmas of where values conflict, to puzzle and worry about them, and in a spirit of pluralism to act according to what seems best in each context, struggling to act well through self-aware judgement which respects the rights and realities of others.

Strikingly, these four themes all point to personal behaviour, attitudes, values and commitment. This is evident in many of the contributions. It applies to all of us who seek to intervene and influence the lives of others, whether through research, facilitation, sensitization or other development actions. In offsetting biases, this means working for gender equity, reducing dominance by men, and meeting, listening to and learning from women in places and at times they find convenient. In the local context it means being sensitive to social diversity and complexity in various dimensions of social difference, including, though not exclusively, gender. In conflict it means being alert and exercising good judgement in facilitating and managing process and mediating negotiation, resolving differences and nurturing relationships in which those who lose in one way gain in others. In ethical issues, it means consulting women, girls and others who are weak, and continual self-questioning, not to the point of paralysis, but reflecting on values, combining commitment with being open to self-doubt, and learning and changing oneself.

It is in this spirit that personal sensitivity pervades this book. The insights into gender relations and into participation are nuanced. The presentations are balanced, insightful and persuasive. The experience, evidence and analysis are often fascinating, recognizing and celebrating differences. The tensions and difficulties encountered with gender have generated concepts, methods and understandings which are subtle, and which ground participation in a deeper realism.

Now that we have this book, it deserves the widest distribution and readership. For those who specialize in gender, it opens up participation. For those who specialize in participation, it reinforces the gender dimension in full measure. For all other development professionals – whether academics, researchers or trainers, whether field practitioners, managers, consultants or policy-makers, and whether in government organizations, bilateral or multilateral donor agencies, or international or national NGOs – it offers readable access to new development needs and opportunities.

The Myth of Community takes us – development professionals – a long step forward. After this, 'gender' and 'participation' can never be quite the same again. Let me hope that this book will be read, reread and reflected on, and that its insights will permeate and help to transform development practice. The editors and authors would never claim to have made a final or definitive statement. They have, though, covered so much new ground so well and so convincingly that the good impact of their work should be deep and lasting. In our world, hundreds of millions are marginalized, oppressed and made miserable by domination and exclusion. Most of them are women. May those who read this book be inspired to act to reduce their marginalization, oppression and misery and to help relations between women and men change for the better. For gender equity and participation have, together, a huge potential for enhancing well-being for all.

Source: Guijt, I. and Shah, M. K. (1998) *Myth of Community: Gender issues in participatory development.* Rugby: Practical Action Publishing, http://doi.org/10.3362/9781853394218

Reflections from Andrea Cornwall

> Andrea Cornwall is Professor of Global Development and Anthropology at King's College London. She first met Robert at one of the legendary RRA methods sharing workshops at IDS in the late 1980s and became a colleague and co-mischief-maker in the Participation Group at IDS in the late 1990s. Her publications include The Participation Reader *(Zed 2011) and – inspired by Robert's care with words –* Buzzwords and Fuzzwords *(Oxfam 2010, co-edited with Deborah Eade).*

The Myth of Community was a landmark in the literature on participatory development. Over the course of the decade before it was published, critiques had begun to emerge from within and outside the community of PRA practitioners that focused on how an undifferentiated notion of 'the community' or 'local people' worked to obscure difference, especially of gender. This book went beyond critique to offer a rich array of lessons and experiments from the world of practice.

Robert's foreword highlights a pervasive thread in his writings: the importance of the personal; the need for reflexivity about biases and assumptions; and the changes in attitudes and behaviour needed for participatory development to be genuinely inclusive and transformative. He speaks of the tendency in participatory development practice to marginalize the voices of women and the need to go beyond naive assumptions about community coherence. But he also goes further than this to pose questions that go much deeper. In his commentary, he also draws attention to questions of politics and ethics, from whether outsiders' interventions are a form of cultural domination, to the role of conflict in social transformation.

Looking back, to have someone as influential as Robert take on board the critique the book articulates and celebrate its lessons was powerful. In the years to come, Robert showed his unfailing commitment to the more inclusive, nuanced approach to participation spelled out in its pages. One of my favourite memories of this was a picture he proudly showed me of him with a group of trans sex workers at an AIDS conference; they'd dressed him up, he was laughing and joking with them, thoroughly comfortable in their presence. It spoke of his deep regard, dignity, and respect for every human being, whoever they were. This shines through in this foreword, which brims with Robert's characteristic excitement about finding out something new and commitment to harnessing creativity for a better world.

Foreword to *Stepping Forward: Children and young people's participation in the development process* (1998) edited by Victoria Johnson, Edda Ivan-Smith, Gill Gordon, Pat Pridmore, and Patta Scott

> Stepping Forward *is an edited book which argued that children should be taken seriously in participatory practice and research. The book documented and reflected on numerous examples of adults facilitating children's participation.*

Participation has entered the mainstream vocabulary of development; inclusion is following hard on its heels. Though practice has lagged behind rhetoric, more and more social groups have been identified as marginal or excluded, and their participation and inclusion seen as priorities. So it has been with women, poor people, ethnic and religious minorities, refugees, the disabled, and the very old. While this has been happening, many have seen children as a different sort of category. Children's health, nutrition and education have long been on the agenda but not their active participation as partners in development.

In part this has reflected the views adults and teachers commonly hold of children and of the young. They are seen as ignorant – to be taught; irresponsible – to be disciplined; immature – to be 'brought up'; incapable – to be protected; a nuisance – 'to be seen and not heard'; or a resource – to be made use of. The pervasive powerlessness of children sustains and reinforces these views; female children or those from low social groups are especially disadvantaged and looked down upon.

With the authority of experience, this book turns these views on their heads. Many old beliefs and attitudes about children cannot survive the evidence presented here: again and again, in different cultures and in whatever context – school, communities or the family, whether as pupils, street children, child labourers or refugees – children are shown to be social actors, with evidence that their capabilities have been underestimated and their realities undervalued.

Appreciating the potentials of children's participation has taken time. An example is the evolution of PRA (participatory rural appraisal) over the past decade. At first, children and younger people were little noticed, even a nuisance. Sometimes they were neutralized by being given something to do – fetching leaves of different trees, or different grasses, or drawing with chalks or pens – to make them useful, keep them quiet or simply for fun. But soon they demonstrated that they could do more than adults supposed. Like older people, they too could make maps, matrices and diagrams. Moreover these showed that their knowledge, realities, preferences and priorities were valid, and differed from those of women and men. Like other 'lowers' they, too, could be empowered to express and analyse their realities and present them to 'uppers'.

Stepping Forward brings together many other illustrations. The experiences described open up a new and wonderful world in which adults facilitate more than teach, and children show that they can do much more than adults thought they could. So we have here children's participation not just in their own social groups but in conferences, councils and community meetings; children's planning and analysis using techniques of mapping, diagramming and matrix scoring; children as researchers; children taking photographs and videos to document their lives; and children designing and performing their own drama, radio broadcasts and television programmes.

For many of us adults, this is more than an ordinary book. It is an invitation to see and relate to children in new ways. The change of view can be compared with becoming aware of gendered roles and attitudes. It demonstrates how much our mindsets about children, like those about gender roles, are socially constructed and reproduced through power relations.

There is, though, a difference. With gender-awareness there have been many adults, mostly women, able and willing to speak out for themselves and others. For children, in contrast, this is rarely possible. In cultures of adult power it is difficult for them to assert themselves, being as they are at once smaller, weaker, more dependent, less articulate, and less able to meet and organize.

For their reality to be recognized and to count they have then to rely on sensitive insight and enabling by adults. These qualities in adults, though still not common, are shown in full measure by the contributors to this book. Working separately in 30 countries spread through five continents, they have explored similar terrain and made similar discoveries. They have faced similar ethical issues in facilitating children's participation. Coming together in the workshop which gave rise to this book, their experiences generated synergy and an infectious excitement. These are now shared in a measured and balanced manner with a wider audience. Richly diverse in culture and context, the findings converge on striking conclusions: that children across the world can do more, and be more creative, than most adults believe; that children's knowledge, perceptions and priorities often differ from what adults suppose them to be; and that giving children space and encouragement to act and express themselves is doubly fulfilling, with rewards for children and adults alike. So this is a book not just about the participation of children and young people. It is also about new forms of fulfilment for adults, the rewards of sharing power and of enabling those who are younger to discover and express more of their potential.

Let me hope that when our children look back from later in the 21st century, they will see this book as part of a watershed in adult understanding and behaviour towards the young. There is perhaps no more powerful way of transforming human society than changing how the adults of today relate to children, the adults of tomorrow. By sharing their explorations and experiences with children and young people, the contributors and editors of *Stepping Forward* have done good service. Their new understandings of children will make many other adults want to change. Their contributions invite us to join them on a steep learning curve. For this, their insights give us a flying start, for they show us how we can enable children to participate and be included more as partners in development; how we can see, relate to and empower them in new ways; and how we can help them discover for themselves more of their remarkable potentials. The message I take from this book is that if we adults can only change our views and behaviour, children will astonish us with what they can do, be and become, and how in time they can make our world a better place.

Source: Johnson, V., Ivan-Smith, E., Gordon, G., Pridmore, P. and Scott, P. (1998) *Stepping Forward: Children and young people's participation in the development process*. Rugby: Practical Action Publishing, http://doi.org/10.3362/9781780443478

Reflections from Michael Gibbons

Michael Gibbons has worked in education, community development, and social justice since the mid-1970s in Asia, Africa, Latin America, and low-income areas of the USA. He designs and facilitates cooperative learning, capacity building, and social justice efforts and helps build collaboration and learning networks. He is a founding member of The Alternatives Project, building a global critical voice to advance new forms of regenerative education and social transformation. Robert Chambers' work inspired and guided decades of his work in agricultural extension, non-formal education, and decolonizing development.

Robert Chambers has always helped us see and acknowledge the inherent dignity and capacity of people deemed by others as inferior. He has also relentlessly demanded, in his humble, plain-spoken way, that we acknowledge and address the fundamental power differences that disadvantage some people and privilege others, and the socially constructed mindsets that justify these unequal power relations. His thinking, analysis, and guidance for transforming practice were way ahead of their time and, while often ignored or resisted, have stood the test of time as ethical and moral guidance in difficult and contentious times. He is an important prophet of greater recognition, inclusion, and participation in our unequal world.

In his foreword to *Stepping Forward: Children and young people's participation in the development process*, published in 1998, Chambers applied this thinking directly to adult relations with children. He made the case that children are a group whose dignity and capacity we underestimate, who we therefore deem inferior, and over whom we exercise unequal power, to our and their great detriment. He outlined succinctly and concretely several of the key tenets of the mindset now called 'adultism', defined as the power adults have over children; the prejudice justifying adult social control of children; the bias toward adult views and needs as the ordering principles of the social world (Flasher, 1978; Fletcher, 2015; Gregoire and Jungers, 2007). He argued that *Stepping Forward* signals a powerful departure from this perspective, documenting numerous examples of child participation across the world and in many fields of endeavour. Chambers endorses the book by saying: 'For many of us adults, this is more than an ordinary book. It is an invitation to see and relate to children in new ways.'

In 1986, David Morley and Hermione Lovel from the Institute of Child Health at the University of London's Teaching Aids at Low Cost programme published a powerful illustrated discussion book called *My Name is Today* about the central role of child wellbeing in the pursuit of just societies. This book spoke powerfully *for* children, a key step of 'recognition' of children in development. In this foreword 12 years later, Chambers pointed out that *Stepping Forward* went further, powerfully laying out the necessity and opportunity for children to *speak for themselves*, showcasing numerous examples of child 'inclusion' and 'participation' supported by shifts in adults' perspective and behaviour. In a UNICEF policy booklet published for the new millennium in 2000, children express their views *first* in a statement called 'A World Fit for Us' before the adult advocates of child rights and dignity weigh in with their commitments to foster *A World Fit for Children* – 'inclusion' and 'participation' encoded as a global policy norm. In 2018, *Children's Participation in Global Contexts: Going beyond voice* signalled further progress in going beyond a call just for children's representation and voice to more direct involvement in action for change. More recently, a set of new efforts to push these boundaries even further has emerged:

- The REJUVENATE Project that documents, archives, and exchanges worldwide examples of creative and daring child advocacy, action, and accountability work (Johnson et al., 2020; Lewin et al. 2023).
- The Child Rights Innovation Fund experiments with funding child- and youth-led development, rights, and justice efforts, and engaging children and youth in the grant-making process itself.
- The Climate Champions Invention Challenge co-hosted by The Rights Studio, Child Rights International Network, and Little Inventors.org helps children invent solutions to components of the climate crisis.

Robert Chambers' foreword to *Stepping Forward* a quarter of a century ago encouraged this gathering wave of child and youth participation and wove it tightly into the fabric of our enduring efforts to redress power differences in our unequal world, dignifying children and young people as fundamental actors in our collective quest for justice.

References

Flasher, J. (1978). Adultism. *Adolescence* 13 (51): 517–23. PMID 735921.

Fletcher, A. (2015). *Facing Adultism*. Olympia, WA: CommonAction Publishing.

Gregoire, J. and Jungers, C.M. (2007). *The Counsellor's Companion*, London: Routledge p. 65.

Johnson, V., Lewin, T., and Cannon, M. (2020). *Learning from a Living Archive: Rejuvenating child and youth rights and participation*, REJUVENATE Working Paper 1. Brighton: Institute of Development Studies.

Lewin, T., Cannon, M., Johnson, V., Philip, R. and Raghavan, P. (2023). *Participation For, With, and By Girls: Evidencing impact*, REJUVENATE Working Paper 2. Brighton: Institute of Development Studies.

Forewords to *Who Changes? Institutionalizing participation in development* (1998) edited by James Blackburn and Jeremy Holland, and *Whose Voice?* (1998) edited by Jeremy Holland

Edited by two well-known practitioners and thinkers, Who Changes? *is a book that grapples with the coming of age of participatory approaches, and details many of the challenges of its institutionalization.*

Whose voice? *is a book in three parts – the first exploring case studies in which participatory approaches have been used to influence policy, the second on Participatory Poverty Analysis, and the third, addressing the key themes that emerged in a workshop on the Institutionalization of Participatory Approaches held at the Institute of Development Studies in 1996.*

Jeremy Holland describes these two books as twin volumes, and has reflected on both together after Robert's forewords on each, which we include here.

Who Changes? Institutionalizing participation in development (*1998*)

For us – development professionals in whatever roles, the sort of people who will have a chance to read this book – this is a good time to be alive. Much that we have believed has proved wrong; and a new agenda is fast taking form. As *Who Changes?* shows, this promises, for all of us, whoever we are, whatever our profession or discipline, and wherever we work, the challenge and exhilaration of exploration, innovation, learning, and doing better.

The context

This excitement can be seen in historical context. From the 1950s through the 1960s and 1970s, in the prevailing orthodoxies of development, it was professionals who had the answers. In general we were right and we were the solution. Poor and local people were the problem, and much of the problem was to be solved by education and the transfer of technology. Increasingly, that ideology has been questioned and undermined. The balance has shifted. Development imposed from the top down was often not sustained. More and more we have been recognized as much of the problem, and their participation as the key to sustainability and many of the solutions.

So participation has become a central theme in development. It is new orthodoxy in the World Bank, where it is being mainstreamed: the Bank now has flagship participation projects, and projects are monitored for their degree of participation. An Inter-Agency Learning Group on Participation has been meeting, comprising major multilateral and bilateral donor agencies and some NGOs. In more and more countries and sectors, participation is required in projects and programmes. The lexicon of development has expanded, perhaps irreversibly, to include participation. And as usual with concepts which gain currency, rhetoric has run far, far ahead of understanding, let alone practice.

Requiring participation has preceded a full understanding of its implications. At first, much of the official thinking was that participation was cost-effective: with participation, local people do more; projects cost less; and achievements are more sustainable. So participation has been written into project documents, policies, and even, as in Bolivia, laws. There can be, though, a big gap between requirement and reality. For as this book shows, the changes needed extend back up hierarchies to include the cultures, procedures, incentives, rewards, and recruitment and staffing policies, of NGOs and of government and donor agencies.

One source of learning has been experiences with participatory rural appraisal (PRA). This has evolved rapidly as a mindset, a philosophy, and a repertoire of methods. The essence of PRA is changes and reversals –of role, behaviour, relationship and learning. Outsiders do not dominate and lecture; they facilitate, sit down, listen, watch and learn. Outsiders do not transfer technology; instead they share methods which local people can use for their own appraisal, analysis, planning, action, monitoring and evaluation. Outsiders hand over the stick, trusting the capabilities of local people. The methods help: many involve visualizations – mapping, diagramming, estimating, ranking, scoring and the like – by local people. Beyond the methods, and as contributors to this book state again and again, personal behaviour and attitudes are crucial. Nor are new participatory methods and changes in personal behaviour and attitudes enough on their own. Repeatedly, PRA has encountered barriers to good performance, and to spread, which are institutional.

PRA only began to emerge in the late 1980s and early 1990s, but its spread has been exponential, to over 100 countries and into most domains of rural and urban development. It has been adopted by many government agencies and NGOs. As PRA and participation have become popular, they have been demanded and required often at short notice and on a huge scale. The results have often been bad. At the same time, in some cases where introduction has been gradual, with good training, sustained support and institutional change, the results have been profoundly encouraging.

Learning from these experiences has become urgent and vital. Recognizing this, the Institute of Development Studies, Sussex, through support from Swiss Development Cooperation, convened a workshop on Institutionalization of Participatory Approaches. On 16 and 17 May 1996, some 50 people from 26 countries took part. The papers and discussions, with James Blackburn as the main editor, provide the core of this book, updated and augmented by new material from this rapidly evolving field. Another workshop a few days earlier drew together experience on PRA and policy. A companion volume, *Whose Voice?*, with Jeremy Holland as the main editor, similarly presents and analyses much learning from recent experience in a new field. It finds that PRA and related participatory approaches have opened up new ways in which policy can be influenced by the realities of those who are poor, weak, marginalized and excluded. Thematic studies in a participatory mode, and broader participatory poverty assessments, have revealed new insights with policy implications. *Whose Voice?* and *Who Changes?* are part of a sequence of publications which draw on PRA-related experience.

Lessons being learnt

The contributions to *Who Changes?* are a rich harvest of experience and judgement. They represent a stage in a process of learning. Most of the authors have been engaged in practical work over at least a decade. Though drawing on experiences from different contexts, countries and continents, they converge strikingly on similar insights and issues. The lessons are convincing but cannot be final. Perhaps there can never be closure on any conventional wisdom in such a dynamic and complex field. In five or ten years' time, more will be known, other lessons will have been learnt, and what we believe we have learnt now will have been qualified and added to by further experience.

All the same, two strong working conclusions stand out as basic and likely to last. They are that:

- sustained participation in development demands transformations in three domains: methods and procedures; institutional cultures; and personal behaviour and attitudes. All three are needed. Each reinforces the others. Each presents points of entry for change,
- of these, personal behaviour and attitudes are crucial. Participation is about how people interact. Dominating behaviour inhibits participation. Democratic behaviour to enable and empower encourages it. For those with power and authority to adopt non-dominating, empowering behaviour almost always entails personal change.

Frontiers now

Many of the frontiers now are practical, about how to make good change happen. They concern methodology – how to do things better, and research – how to learn from experience. The contributors to this book give us a flying start, with readable accounts and practical analysis. Readers of the book may wish to draw up and act on their own lists of priorities. To me, after reading the book, five stand out:

- *Training.* How better to conduct training for attitude and behaviour change, the ABC of PRA (Kumar 1996); how sympathetically to help those threatened by participatory modes of interaction; how best to arrange programmes of total immersion in villages and slums as learning experiences for powerful people (as being implemented for its senior staff by the World Bank), and how to spread this practice; and how to assure continuity of training as part of a long-term process.
- *Going to scale.* How optimally to balance drives to go too fast and brakes to go too slow; how to assess, improve and insert 'benign viruses' in going to scale, elements like behaviour and attitude training, embracing error, reflection and critical self-awareness which have self-improvement built in; and how to insist on small pilots for testing and learning, with only gradual scaling-up at a measured pace.
- *Institutional change.* How to change the cultures and procedures of hierarchical organizations, whether donor agencies, government departments, or larger NGOs; how to overcome the common conflict between low level corruption and participation; how to avoid the tyranny of targets and drives for disbursements; how to select participatory staff and achieve a gender balance; how to protect and retain good staff and participation when there is a backlash; how to reward participatory work; how to help middle managers who resist change; and how to assure continuity of support at the top.
- *Participatory monitoring and evaluation.* How to complete the participation circle by enabling groups and communities to conduct their own M and E, with their own baselines and indicators; and how to reconcile this with central needs for standard indicators and information.
- *Disempowerment.* How to enable powerful people to recognize that power is not a commodity to be amassed, but a resource to be shared; and how to enable them to gain satisfaction, fulfilment and even fun, from disempowering themselves and empowering others.

To learn how to do these things better will not be easy. It requires more practitioners and researchers to follow contributors to this book in engaging with and learning from field and organizational realities. Combinations of approach may be best, including PRA, participatory action research, process documentation, participatory monitoring and evaluation, and self-critical reflection. Above all, it is vital to make the effort to share experiences and insights openly and without boundaries: in conversations, writing, and workshops, and through words, diagrams, videos, publications, networking and newsletters. This book provides a baseline of rich experience and insight. The challenge is to make the baseline a springboard, to learn more and to do better. May it inspire others to innovate, research, write and share, to help all of us do better in our understanding and actions.

The central message I draw from the contributions to this book is that participation has to be pervasive. In Andrew Shepherd's phrase (this volume) it cannot be bolted on. It cannot be confined to a low-level ghetto. Any belief that induced participation can succeed on any scale without participatory cultures and practices in the initiating organizations, and without personal change, cannot survive this book. Participation has to be lived, and lived at all levels by all concerned.

So the final frontier remains personal. In earlier decades, it was local people who had to change. Now the imperative has been reversed. The finger now points back to us - development professionals, the sort of people most likely to read these words. The experiences presented here drive us to an uncomfortable truth: that the quality of development depends on what sort of people we are and what we do. The title of this book poses the question **Who Changes?** The answer is inescapable. It has to be us.

Kumar, S. (Ed.) (1996) 'ABC of PRA: attitude and behaviour change', in *Participation, Policy and Institutionalisation*, PLA notes 27, London : IIED.

Whose voice? (1998)

Whose Voice? presents a dramatic learning: it is that now, in the last years of the twentieth century, we have new ways in which those who are poor and marginalized can present their realities to those in power, and be believed, influence policy and make a difference.

The context

To many readers this will seem improbable. We live, after all, in a world of increasing polarization of power and wealth into North and South, into overclasses and underclasses. Materially, those in the overclasses have more and more, and are increasingly linked by instant communications. At the same time, the numbers in the underclasses of absolute poverty continue to rise. Among them, many millions have less and less, and remain isolated both from the overclass and from each other. Almost by definition, the poor and powerless have no voice. It may be politically correct to say that they should be empowered and their voices heard. But cynical realists will point to inexorable trends, vested interests and pervasive self-interest among the powerful, and argue that little can be changed.

The contributors to this book present evidence of new potentials to the contrary. They confront that cynicism with their own promising experience. They have found that there are new ways to enable those who are poor, marginalized, illiterate and excluded to analyse their realities and express their priorities; that the realities they express of conditions, problems, livelihood strategies and priorities often differ from what development professionals have believed; and that new experiences can put policymakers in closer touch with those realities.

These potentials come from participatory research in which the poor themselves are active analysts. This has a long pedigree, not least in the traditions of participatory action research and the inspiration of Paulo Freire and his followers. In the late 1980s and early 1990s a confluence of older streams of research together with new inventions evolved as a family of approaches and methods known as participatory rural appraisal (PRA). This has spread fast and wide. It is now often urban and frequently much more than appraisal. It has been applied in all continents, and many countries and contexts.

PRA stresses changes in the behaviour and attitudes of outsiders, to become not teachers but facilitators, not lecturers but listeners and learners. 'Hand over the stick', 'Use your own best judgement at all times' and 'They can do it' (having confidence in the abilities of local people, whether literate or not) are among its sayings. When well conducted, PRA approaches and methods are often open-ended, visual as well as verbal, and carried out by small groups of local people. They have proved powerful means of enabling local people, including the poor, illiterate, women and the marginalized, themselves to appraise, analyse, plan and act. While some consider that PRA should always be part of an empowering process, others have used the methods for research, to learn more and more accurately about the realities of the poor.

As PRA evolved, it soon became evident that it had applications for policy. Thematic and sectoral studies were carried out and presented as reports to decision makers, sometimes in only days or weeks from the fieldwork. The World Bank, through trust funds from bilateral donors, initiated participatory poverty assessments (PPAs). Some of these used PRA methods to enable poor people to express their realities themselves. The insights from these thematic studies and PPAs were often striking, convincing and unexpected. A quiet revolution was taking place in parallel in different parts of the world, but it was too scattered for full mutual learning or for its significance to be fully seen.

Through support from Swiss Development Cooperation, an international workshop was convened at the Institute of Development Studies, University of Sussex, over the two days 13–14 May 1996, to share and review relevant experience with PRA and policy. Some 50 participants of 26 nationalities took part. The papers and discussions from that workshop, with Jeremy Holland as the main editor, provide the core of this book, updated and augmented by new material from this rapidly evolving field.

A related workshop a few days later drew together experience on the institutionalizing of participatory approaches. A companion volume, *Who Changes?* with James Blackburn as the main editor, similarly presents and analyses much learning from recent experience. It finds that PRA and related participatory approaches have presented many challenges – ethical, institutional and personal, especially as they go to scale with large organizations. It concludes with a bottom line that how good development is depends on what sort of people 'we' – development professionals – are. *Who Changes?* and *Whose Voice?* are part of a sequence of publications which draw on PRA-related experience.

In reading *Whose Voice?* there is excitement to be found, and a certain exhilaration. For one realizes gradually that there has been a breakthrough. Many questions are raised. Among these, certain insights and issues stand out and deserve comment, among these methods and ethics and the realities revealed.

Methods and ethics

With participatory research, and especially with PRA, methods and ethics are intertwined; issues raised are of time taken, expectations aroused and whose realities are expressed. Several writers agonize over whether the research process is exploitative. Participatory research is time-consuming for local people: PRA methods, especially the visual ones like mapping, diagramming and matrices, tend to be fun and to engage people's full attention, but sometimes for hours; and poor people's time is not costless. Expectations are also liable to be raised.

After being helped to analyse their conditions, problems and opportunities, people often expect action, but with facilitators in a policy research mode, and not concerned with planning for action, follow-up may not be feasible.

No solutions can be universal, but two points are widely agreed:

- Transparency: facilitators should make clear from the start who they are, what they are doing, and why, and what can and cannot be expected; often, even when nothing can be expected, local people will collaborate, not least because they find the activities interesting and enjoyable, and themselves learn from them.
- Selection for follow-up: communities and groups can be chosen where responsible follow-up may be possible through an on-going programme.

A further concern is whose reality is being presented, and whose reality counts. Those most accessible to outsiders in communities are usually men, and those who are less poor, less marginalized, less excluded. Women are often continuously busy. Ensuring that the excluded are included, and that their reality is expressed, can demand patience, persistence, tact and inconvenience. The best times for poor women are, for example, often the worst times for outsiders.

There is then the question of how their reality is analysed, and into whose categories. (Researchers tend to fit material into preconceived concepts.) The Management Committee of the South African PPA set an example of best practice by going to pains not to impose their categories and constructs on the material. Instead, through card sorting, they allowed the categories and constructs to emerge from the material, and then to influence the structure of the report, which they wrote as spokespersons for the poor.

Realities revealed

Much of the power of PRA methods lies in what has been called group–visual synergy. Group activities include: making maps, lists, matrices, causal and linkage diagrams, estimating, comparisons, ranking and scoring, and discussing and debating. Realities are expressed in a cumulative physical and visual form, often democratically, on the ground. Typically, people become committed to the process and lose themselves in it.

Visually, more diversity and complexity are expressed than can be put into words. Much in the contributions to this book was first presented visually. The realities revealed in both the thematic studies and the PPAs are often striking. Once stated they seem obvious, but it is sobering to recognize that for urban-based professionals they have usually been new insights, or understanding presented with new force and credibility.

To take examples in turn from the thematic studies:

- In Nepal, in the Tarai (plains) area, the continuous introduction of irrigation and of new crop varieties led to yield increases, but was masking long-term declines in soil fertility.
- In Guinea, contrary to officials' views, indigenous land-tenure systems persisted and were complex and diverse.
- In The Gambia, 25 per cent of girls of school age were found to be overlooked at the village level because they were pregnant, married or about to be married; girls cared deeply and bitterly about the denial of education.
- In Jamaica, poverty and violence are interconnected in complex ways, including area stigma, which hinders those from a neighbourhood with a reputation for violence from getting jobs; interpersonal violence is far more common than political or drug-related violence.
- In India, local people understood the ecology of a national park better than conservation-minded professionals; excluding buffaloes in the name of conservation both damaged their livelihoods and led to a decrease in bird life in the park.

The PPAs were similarly revealing: in Ghana, infrastructure was found to be a higher priority for rural people than had been recognized; in Zambia, school fees had to be paid at the worst time of the year, coinciding with high incidence of sickness and hard work, and shortages of money and food; in South Africa, seasonal deprivation, urban as well as rural, was more significant than had been supposed; in Bangladesh, in a subsequent PPA sponsored by UNDP, enforcement of anti-dowry laws was a surprise priority of poor people. These are illustrative examples from reports rich in policy-relevant detail. The evidence is abundant that these approaches and methods, used well, elicit insights into previously hidden realities of the poor.

Whose Voice? deserves to be read, studied and acted upon by all who are concerned with poverty and policy, in whatever context, country or continent. Its lessons transcend the boundaries of professions, disciplines, sectors and departments. It indicates actions open to NGOs, governments and all agencies concerned with deprivation and with development.

It shares seminal experiences, rather than set answers. It is for readers to select from these what makes sense for their purposes, and to go further themselves.

Let me hope that this book will encourage and inspire many others to join the pioneers who write here, to explore more of this new territory, and to share their experiences with the same disarming frankness. It may then be that the voices and realities of those who have been last – the poor, powerless, marginalized and excluded – will come to count and to change policy both in principle and in practice.

Source: Blackburn, J. and Holland, J. (eds.) (1998) *Who Changes? Institutionalizing participation in development*. Rugby: Practical Action Publishing, http://doi.org/10.3362/9781780446417

Source: Holland, J. with Blackburn, J. (eds.) (1998) *Whose Voice? Participatory research and policy change*. Rugby: Practical Action Publishing, http://doi.org/10.3362/9781780446431

Reflections from Jeremy Holland

> *Jeremy Holland likes being inventive with research methodologies and has a particular interest in participatory approaches that draw on qualitative and combined methods. He has worked as a consultant for a wide range of organizations in developing and transitional countries, from the World Bank and UN agencies and government aid departments through to international and national NGOs. Previously he lectured at the Centre for Development Studies at Swansea University and was a Visiting Fellow at IDS Sussex. He has written about research tools and frameworks, including books on political and social analysis, combined methods, and participatory statistics.*

When I presented Robert with a draft copy of *Whose Voice?* he gently pointed out with a wry smile that I had misspelled 'Foreword' as 'Forward'. How wonderful that we are now using this play on words to reflect on Robert's contribution to an evolving field. *Whose Voice?* and its accompanying volume *Who Changes?*, edited by my late friend and colleague James Blackburn, were the result of two 1996 Swiss Development Cooperation-funded IDS workshops that brought together a global cast of participatory development colleagues.

These two volumes, distilled from the workshop papers and accompanying sense-making discussions, spoke to twin objectives. The first was to challenge and dismantle the institutional cultures and personal behaviours that underpin 'top-down' development (*Who Changes?*). The second was to recognize and privilege, 'bottom-up', the voices and expert analysis of those who are not usually heard by the powerful, with ambition stretched from community-level PRA origins to engagement in 'higher-level' programme and policy processes (*Whose Voice?*).

The workshops were held at a significant moment when participation rhetoric had gained a foothold in aid agencies, notably in the World Bank, which was using bilateral trust funds to generate a flurry of participatory poverty assessments. At the same time community development projects such as the prototype Kecamatan Development Program in Indonesia had gained currency. Robert was duly invited to the Bank, where, in a corporate meeting room that no doubt screamed 'normal professionalism', he distributed thick manuals with a front cover title along the lines of 'how to do participatory development' to each of the assembled divisional heads. The manuals were filled with nothing but empty pages. Robert's subsequent institutional and personal experience of working on the Bank's *Voices of the Poor* project is itself the stuff of legend.

Over the 25 years since the publication of these two collected volumes, development funders have evolved quite sophisticated debates around learning reversal and the institutionalization of participatory development. Discussion, for instance, around 'beneficiary assessments' that rhetorically shift beneficiaries from passive objects of development to active subjects of their own development is a testament to this. More recently, the institutional relevance and potential of this learning reversal framing has been given encouraging new life by the emergence of progressive strands in international development debates. In the wake of #metoo and #blacklivesmatter, policy-makers in western aid-giving countries have begun to reframe their foreign policy towards the need for contextual understanding driven by a newly found respect for local knowledge. The Australian Government, for example, is about to publish a policy paper that repositions its policy approach in the Indo-Pacific region in these terms. At the same time, 'feminist' has emerged as a more widely used adjective among donors, spooked by a powerful social movement that has highlighted the toxicity of patriarchy and masculine culture. Acronyms such as GEDSI (gender equality, disability, and social inclusion), while often painfully articulated and bureaucratically implemented, nonetheless signal an awakening of sorts towards the primacy of the local and the need to drive forward inclusiveness and 'leave no one behind'. There is fertile ground for the long-term, continuing influence of the participatory development experience that was collated in *Who Changes?* and *Whose Voice?*

Foreword to *In the Hands of the People: Selected papers of Anil C. Shah* (2001)

> Anil Shah was an Indian bureaucrat and then NGO worker whom Robert deeply admired. His book is a collection of papers spanning his very diverse career. He died in 2007. Robert's foreword is followed by a piece by Sachin Oza, who worked closely with Anil.

It is a privilege to be invited to contribute a foreword to this collection of the remarkable writings of Shri Anil C. Shah, or Anilbhai as he is so widely known to colleagues and friends. It is exciting, even astonishing, to see them brought together in one cover. Only now is it possible to appreciate the extraordinary range and practical and intellectual value of his work. Unique is not a word to be used lightly, yet to my knowledge this book is unique and stands alone. At once it presents the experience of a life committed to those who are poor and marginalised; it covers an extraordinary range of activities; it stands out for its honesty, perceptiveness and originality; it is based on a bedrock of realism, of direct personal experience and innovation in the field and with poor people; and it shows how participatory action research can feed into policy influence. It contains both short cameos with the telling detail of personal experience, in effect like extracts from a reflective diary, and longer articles which stand back and take a broader view. And it does this from an impressive range of contexts and experiences from government administration to NGOs, from community development to joint forest management, from watershed development to participatory irrigation management, and from behaviour, attitudes and training to influencing and changing policy.

Like the author himself, this book spans the worlds of Government and of civil society. It is informed by a distinguished career in both these fields. In Government, Anilbhai held many posts, from BDO [block development officer] to Secretary of the Government of Gujarat, with responsibilities among others for Administrative Reforms and Training, and for Rural Development. On retirement from Government, he entered the NGO sector formally when he became the Chief Executive of the Aga Khan Rural Support Programme, India. He held that position from 1984 to 1993. He founded the Development Support Centre soon after and has been its Chairman till date. His experience in both Government and civil society, and the respect with which he is held in both, have enabled him to live, work and move equally freely in those two domains which are so often antagonistic. This has given him scope, exploited to the full, to influence both NGO practice and government policy. There is much talk nowadays of advocacy and policy influence but much less understanding of how it can be done, and who is best placed to do it. There are answers to be found in the examples in this book. But the reader who wishes to do likewise, should be warned. For what cannot be conveyed in writing is Anilbhai's personal commitment, energy, patience, tenacity, attention to detail, imagination and sheer ability which led to the achievements so modestly presented here and to many others which are not described.

It is a startling lesson to development professionals, whether in Government, NGOs or research institutions, to note the originality of many of the insights and actions described in these writings. Many of them had been neither recognised nor recorded by others. At the time when they were written up many of them were new in substance and in their implications for policy. An essential source of this originality was engagement in the field. We see here a Government officer, and then the Chief Executive of an NGO, working directly with people and communities, often in the mode of direct field experience through action research. One example is the understanding that for farmers' irrigation societies to become viable, water charges had to be higher, not lower, and the way in which this was followed through into a simple, but radical and transforming change of policy. Another is the famous Government Order of 1 June 1990, so widely influential in many parts of India, which empowered village communities and voluntary agencies to combine to regenerate degraded forest lands. These changes could not have been achieved by academic research alone, nor by NGOs alone, nor indeed by Government alone. It needed someone engaged with action in the field, sensitively aware of local people's realities, and with access to and understanding of Government, to be able to see what change was needed and how it might be achieved. Most development professionals are trapped in one domain, with one set of perspectives. From Anilbhai we can come to appreciate the huge gains that can be made by working and engaging at the same time in three domains – with poor people, with civil society, and with Government, and bringing all their perspectives together for mutual learning and change.

There is much else to ponder in this book: about the powerlessness of those who are poor and marginalised, and how they can be empowered; about gainers and losers in development, and how again and again sensitive understanding can find ways for losers to become gainers; about how the exclusion of women and neglect of their priorities and interests can be reversed; about how the perceptions and priorities of professionals so often differ from those of farmers and local people; about how professionals can unlearn and learn; and in some of the most revealing passages in this book, about sequences and skills in discussions with poor people.

One theme that runs through many of these papers deserves special note. It concerns participatory behaviours and attitudes and the radical changes these often require of us. Anilbhai was one of the outstanding pioneers of the methods, approaches, behaviours and attitudes of PRA (Participatory Rural Appraisal). From the beginning, he recognised and emphasised that, to use his own words, "right attitudes and behaviour are at the heart of participation". It is one thing to read, speak and write about friendly behaviour, active listening, a learning attitude, and avoiding critical remarks, lecturing, preaching and the like. It is quite another to practise these things. What the reader cannot see, but can sense from some of the dialogue, is Anilbhai's own sensitivity and skill as a facilitator in the field, sitting and listening, encouraging those who at first are timid, patiently probing, and quietly helping people to explore and analyse their own realities without imposing his.

Above all, through these writings, we are challenged by Anilbhai to see things differently, to act differently, and to relate differently to other people. They speak to all of us who are concerned with development work, whatever our organisations, disciplines or professions, whether as fieldworkers, policy-makers, politicians, administrators, managers, teachers, trainers or students, and whether in Government, NGOs, universities, colleges and training institutes, or the private sector. There is much material here for reflection. And the lessons have a universality: they apply, and the learning is needed, not only in India, nor only in South Asia, but in all countries of the South and North.

We are also invited to learn from and emulate, however modestly, Anilbhai's life of continuous and committed engagement, of doing and learning, and of relationships of empathy and respect with those who are poor and excluded. There is inspiration in the force of his example. It shows how those in Government service can break the mould. It indicates to those who retire from Government service the appropriate attitudes, behaviours and relationships for embarking on a second career. It shows all of us what can be done through understanding the realities of poor people, empowering them, and as faithful allies championing their cause. It tells us not to retire, not to give up, and not to stop.

The message we can take from this book is above all of hope. At a time when cynics and sceptics spread gloom and despair about development we see here the great scope for good things to be done. Denuded land can grow trees; those denied water can receive it; those who are excluded can gain in voice and self-respect. For those who are worst off, the world can become a better place. The quality of their lives and experiences can improve. In innumerable ways, differences can be made. Seemingly small individual actions add up. Big changes can come, as they have done and continue to do, so wonderfully through the life of the author

So let me urge others to read what Anilbhai has written, to be inspired, and to act.

12 December 2001
Robert Chambers

Source: Iyengar, S. and Hirway, I. (eds.) (2001) *In the Hands of the People: Selected papers of Anil C. Shah*. Ahmedabad: Gujarat Institute of Development Research.

Reflections from Sachin Oza

Sachin Oza is currently the Executive Director of DSC Foundation, an organization formed by DSC with a focus on research, documentation, and policy influencing. He has been with DSC since its inception in 1994 and is a practitioner, trainer, and researcher. He worked closely with Anilbhai initially as a Training Coordinator of DSC, then as its Executive Director from 2001 to 2016 and continues to mentor DSC.

The volume *In the Hands of the People* is a compilation of several studies and papers written by Mr Anil C. Shah in 2001. Thereafter he brought out Volume II in 2005. These are a reflection of his long journey of more than 50 years in the government and civil society. He started his career as a bureaucrat in 1952 as a Block Development Officer in the Junagadh district of Gujarat, India and was the Secretary, Rural Development, at the Government of Gujarat in 1980. After his long stint in the government, he had an equally long innings as a practitioner.

In 1984, he became the Chief Executive Officer of the Aga Khan Rural Support Programme (India) (AKRSPI). Under his leadership, AKRSPI focused on enhancing the livelihoods of rural communities through participatory natural resource management in three diverse geographical areas of Gujarat. Within a few years, he built a competent and committed team of professionals that made a remarkable impact on the lives of rural communities by building their capacities to plan, implement, and manage their resources, whether canals, watersheds, or forests. A firm believer in the knowledge of rural communities and their participation, he got in touch with Professor Robert Chambers from IDS, Sussex and was one of the pioneers in promoting Participatory Rural Appraisal (PRA) methods in the country.

In 1994, Anilbhai became the Chairman of the Development Support Centre (DSC). He had long felt that the state and country would need many more NGOs such as AKRSPI if they were to make any real impact. Thus, DSC focused on capacity building, strengthening civil society organizations, and facilitating an enabling environment at the state and national levels. Having served as a policy-maker and as a practitioner, Anilbhai constantly worked towards joining the strengths of government and civil society.

Anilbhai unfortunately passed away in 2007 but DSC continues to carry forward his rich legacy and vision. The organization has expanded its area of operations thematically as well as geographically. Until 2007, DSC operated only in Gujarat and focused on water management. Currently, it is operating in more than 900 villages in Madhya Pradesh, Maharashtra, and Rajasthan. Anilbhai was keen to promote Watershed + and PIM+,[1] interventions related to sustainable agriculture and enterprise development to enhance the incomes of small and marginal farmers. Based on this vision, DSC has developed a unique approach called *Water to Wealth* wherein it initiates interventions related to water management in rainfed and irrigated areas then promotes sustainable agriculture and collective enterprise development through farmer producer organizations. It is recognized as a resource centre at the state and national levels and continues to conduct studies and influence policies through the DSC Foundation. Sajjata Sangh, a network of NGOs in natural resource management in Gujarat that Anilbhai had initiated in 2002, continues to be relevant even now. Similarly, AKRSPI is recognized as one of the leading NGOs in the country. It continues to grow and expand its operational area from Gujarat to Madhya Pradesh, Bihar, and now Maharashtra.

Anilbhai's thinking and vision continue to be embedded in our thoughts and action through some of the path-breaking studies and papers in these volumes, for example: 'The Deprived in the command area of irrigation systems', 'Learning from Farmers', 'Eloquent Silent Revolution', 'More or Less', 'Joining of Strengths', and 'Fading Shine of the Golden Decade – The Establishment Strikes Back'. The studies and papers based on ground-level data and his own experiences provide a glimpse of Anilbhai's flair for writing, reflecting, analysing, and providing critical insights in a simple, lucid, jargon-free manner. They played a major role in influencing government policies and programmes initiated in the early 1990s such as Joint Forest Management, Participatory Watershed Management, and Participatory Irrigation Management. These programmes ushered in a bottom-up approach through active participation of the community in the planning, implementation, and management of their resources.

Two of the most significant contributions made by Anilbhai are the 'Sequential Steps in Empowering Communities: The Cost–Benefit Approach' and the 'Bhopal Declarations – Principles of sustainable natural resource management'. The 'Sequential steps' provide practical guidance to organize the communities through real facilitation and not in a top-down manner. While the Steps are targeted at the practitioners, the Bhopal Declarations are for the policy-makers, and both have universal applicability. If implemented in the right spirit, the Bopal Declarations and Sequential Steps can create a far-reaching impact on the design and operationalization of natural resource management policies not only in India but elsewhere too. They provide valuable insight into how to empower rural communities to plan, implement, and sustainably manage their natural resources. The Sequential Steps show the sensitivity and concern of Anilbhai in reaching the unreached while the Bopal Declarations reflect his vision for designing people-centred natural resource management programmes.

Note

1. Watershed interventions capture rain water where it falls, for later use PIM refers to Participatory Irrigation Management; the plus refers to programme additions, such as capacity building.

Foreword to the Japanese translation of *Participatory Workshops* (2003)

> Robert's workshops are world-famous, particularly among the IDS alumni, many of whom spent their weekends doing unexpected things in Room 221. Andrea Cornwall and Ian Scoones (2011: 7) joke that behind one of the wall hangings in this room was a sign that said 'Robert, put it back' because he so often removed all the pictures from the wall to put up his own workshop charts and drawings. The English edition of Participatory Workshops was published in 2002. I know of many people, in diverse professions, who regard it as a facilitation bible of sorts. Robert's foreword is followed by reflections from Patta Scott-Villiers and Jo Howard who, very bravely, have been trying to keep alive Robert's weekend workshop tradition within IDS.

The rhetoric of development has changed in recent years. It is not just that there is renewed emphasis on poverty. It is also that new words have become prominent. Twenty years ago we heard little about empowerment, partnership, ownership, participation, accountability and transparency. Now these six words are prominent in project proposals, evaluations, annual reports, speeches, and academic studies alike. All six words refer to relationships; all concern power; and all are used hypocritically. We have the words without the behaviours, attitudes and relationships they imply. Top-down, centre-outwards, hierarchical, control-oriented organisations, procedures and relationships have proved robust. While these continue, and while the gaps between words and realities persist, processes of development with and by poor people will continue to be hampered.

To narrow these gaps demands action and change on many fronts. Among these, not least are liberalising bureaucratic procedures and requirements, removing time-bound targets for participatory processes, and evolving more egalitarian and co-equal partnerships. Less well recognised is the need to change behaviours and attitudes. And even less recognised is how vital it is, in the long term, to change approaches and methods in teaching and training. The schools, colleges, universities and training institutes of the world have an enormous effect on those who pass through them. As students and trainees they are conditioned by how they are taught, and then pass out to repeat the behaviour and reproduce the relationships they have experienced. So top-down didactic teaching in classrooms and lecture theatres leads to dominating attitudes and behaviours in the outside world. Graduates are turned out disabled by their experience of education and in immediate need of rehabilitation. If development is to become more genuinely participatory and empowering for the poor, the experiences of being taught and learning must themselves be more participatory. What goes on in schools, colleges, universities and training institutes has to change.

This collection of ideas and activities is intended as a contribution, however modest, to such change. It draws on experiences with PRA/PLA (Participatory Rural Appraisal or Participatory Reflection and Action, and Participatory Learning and Action). Four findings and principles that have been key in those experiences, and which fit here, are:

- Attitude and behaviour change (the ABC of PRA). The basic importance of the behaviour and attitudes of "uppers" – teachers, lecturers, trainers or facilitators.
- They can do it and Handing over the stick. The recognition that "lowers" – students, trainees or participants, usually have a far greater capacity to do things such as appraise, analyse and themselves teach others, than their "uppers" suppose; and that

- Fun. To enjoy activities when possible. The extremes of poverty, discrimination, exclusion, intimidation and violence in the world are awful. But that is no reason for us not to enjoy living. It is all the more reason to help poor people themselves to share in fun and creativity.
- Use your own best judgement at all times, meaning accepting personal responsibility and using personal judgement and initiative rather than relying on a manual.

Which leads to the point that this small volume is a sourcebook, not a manual. My hope is that by showing some of the things that can be done it will encourage more and more teachers, lecturers, facilitators, and convenors and organisers of workshops and conferences to try out new ways of enabling others to learn, share and change. Most of the activities and exercises are quite safe: they are not too difficult to facilitate or to participate in. There is, as ever, a danger that this will be used like a textbook and taken too seriously. What matters most is a spirit of adventure, a willingness to take risks, to "fail forwards", to experiment, innovate, invent and learn on the run. So the reader is referred repeatedly to the 21st of each 21 which is on the lines of "invent for yourself".

There are cultural differences in how we teach and learn. As I make clear in the preface, this is a collection by an Englishman, a condition over which I have no control. Others will judge what is culturally specific and what is more generally applicable. Let anything be adopted or adapted as seems most fitting, given the original intention. Throughout, let it serve as a challenge to all concerned to ask whether there are more participatory and better ways of doing what they do. One question is: do many of the ideas and activities described here have application in higher education? For it is often universities and colleges which are the most conservative, and the last to learn and to change. I believe that there are participatory alternatives to most didactic teaching. A few are presented here. Many more exist or may be waiting to be invented. University and college teachers can ask themselves: "Is your lecture really necessary? Are there better ways to help learners learn?"

Finally, let me thank Naoto Noda for having the idea of making this translation, for having found and coordinated a team of translators, and for having brought the project to completion in such a short time. This has been a remarkable achievement. To him, and to all those others who have taken part:

> Yoshiko Oi
> Hideyo Shimazu
> Yukio Ono
> Ken'ichi Ishida
> Tatsuro Fujikura
> Kiyoshi Shiratori

I ask readers to join me in expressing gratitude, and to thank them face-to-face if you meet them. It cannot have been easy to translate some of my idiosyncratic English. For their commitment, dedication and patience, I thank all those concerned, together with their families who may have seen less of them than they would have wished.

If you see this book, may you find pleasure in it. It is serious, but also meant to be fun. So my final word is an invitation to you all to

ENJOY

15 April 03   Robert Chambers

Source: Kogan Page Ltd through The English Agency (Japan) of Chambers, R. (2002) *Participatory Workshops. A sourcebook of 21 sets of ideas and activities.* London: Routledge.

Source: Cornwall, A. and Scoones, I. (eds.) (2011). Revolutionizing Development: Reflections on the work of Robert Chambers. London: Earthscan.

Reflections from Jo Howard and Patta Scott-Villiers

Jo Howard is a research fellow at IDS where she leads the Participation, Inclusion and Social Change Cluster. She has been fortunate to work alongside Robert and learn participatory skills and principles from him, and from colleagues and partners around the world. Before working in an academic setting, she spent six years teaching, working, and training in Nicaragua. Her research approach is participatory, and she is endlessly inspired by Robert's advice to listen, learn from failure, and learn together.

Patta Scott-Villiers had been supporting women's banking on the Kenya-Somalia border when she came into IDS seeking ideas for participatory approaches. Next thing she knew she was helping Robert to organize a participation resource centre, a place from which people all over the world could find stories, guides, and ways of working that could help them in their efforts to put the last first. Patta now teaches and convenes the Master's degree at IDS on power, participation, and social change and still supports people in the drylands of East Africa to do powerful participatory research.

Robert's book *Participatory Workshops* is an essential sourcebook for our participatory teaching and research. It reminds us of the participatory principles that we teach, and that we aim to embody in our practice.

In our research, we often engage with people who have experienced – and most continue to experience – poverty, discrimination, and marginalization. If they have engaged with government or public services, these have been done 'to them' without offering them space and time to reflect, analyse, and propose. It is an attitude that Robert neatly dissects in his phrase 'uppers and lowers'. In our teaching, we help students to question a certainty that to be formally educated is to be cleverer than those who have not been to school. It's another of Robert's bittersweet observations, that the longer we have been educated, the more we must unlearn.

The movement to promote participation in development has been around for over 50 years in the international development field – Robert was a pioneer. And this movement was inspired by the work of Paolo Freire, Orlando Fals Borda, Myles Horton, and others who were innovating and revolutionizing education and community development in the 1970s (see Ospina et al., 2021). Yet, the principles Robert outlines in his foreword still sit uncomfortably with mainstream teaching and research: adopting attitudes and behaviours which reduce the power of the 'professional'; recognizing and facilitating the capacity of people experiencing marginalization to reflect, analyse, decide, propose, act, and teach others; adopting a flexible approach which is sensitive to context and allows innovation to emerge; and seeing participatory work as fundamentally human, relational, and celebratory of life (having fun, as Robert would say).

In Robert's foreword, he emphasizes the need to model participatory ways of working in our teaching. This is central to how we approach teaching in our Master's in Power, Participation and Social Change at IDS. We avoid the lecture format, and adopt a conversational approach, recognizing that to learn we need to engage with our own and others' experience. We encourage students to facilitate, recognizing that we learn through doing. We use visual methods such as Rivers of Life and mapping, recognizing that we learn and generate new knowledge when we present our knowledge to others through visual media. And we encourage discussion, as through dialogue we generate new ideas. This means that we embed our teaching in an extended epistemology (Heron and Reason, 2008).

Jo says,

> in recent years, I have been increasingly invited to train professionals in aid organizations in PRA methods. Robert's book is a great companion and encouragement in this work. I have found that people have a 'lightbulb' moment when they practise the methods for real, and find that the people become animated, share experiences, work together, and can generate analysis that goes beyond what professionals, looking from the outside inwards, could have done.

Patta says,

> I've worked with pastoralists in East Africa for many years, and their ways of learning from experience, practice, attention and dialogue always remind me of Robert. He often told me how he learned from them in his early days. Their way of speaking is like his, too, very straightforward.

We have felt that Robert is at our shoulders, encouraging us, and that 'have fun!' and 'hand over the stick!' have become embodied. The simplicity of Robert's messages is disarming, and deceptive. The content is in fact profound. In our professional worlds we develop language and procedures that distance us from people and therefore from the change that can only happen if we consider ourselves to be truly equal to all those with whom we interact.

References

Heron, J. and Reason, P. (2008), Extending epistemology within a co-operative inquiry', in Reason, P. and Bradbury, H. (eds) *The SAGE Handbook of Action Research. Participative Inquiry and Practice.* 2nd edition. London: Sage, pp. 365–80

Ospina, S. Burns, D. and Howard, J. (eds) (2021) 'Introduction to the handbook: Navigating the complex and dynamic landscape of participatory research and inquiry', in *The SAGE Handbook of Participatory Research and Inquiry.* Burns, D. Howard, J. and Ospina, S. London: Sage, pp. 3–16.

Draft foreword to *How to Design a Training Course: A guide to participatory curriculum development* (2003) by Peter Taylor

> *Robert's foreword for this book somehow didn't quite make it into the book, which obviously is all the more reason to include it here.*

Formal and informal teaching, training and learning are human universals, vital for empowerment and a good life; and good education is considered a human right. Yet some 125 million children lack any formal education, and for many who have some the quality is very poor. Learning is limited by the top-down nature of much teaching and training. Fortunately, in recent decades, much has been discovered about how to do better, using participatory approaches, methods and behaviours which can enhance learning. More and more, participatory approaches have been introduced in classrooms, courses and workshops. But a vital step has often been missing. What is to be covered, has been designed by the teacher, trainer or facilitator: the many and varied stakeholders in the process, including the participants, have been little consulted or involved, or not at all. This guide shows us now how important that extra step is and how to take it. For all of us engaged in teaching, training and facilitation, or in sponsoring or supporting education, courses or workshops, here is a source of insight, ideas and advice on how to make the development and design of curriculum and content itself participatory, and teaching and training much more effective.

A major message is that preparation needs more time, patience, participation and adaptability than has been common in the past. This requires more resources. The evidence in these pages is abundant that it pays off handsomely to make available the extra time and resources needed. The impact on any reader who is a teacher, trainer or facilitator may be as immediate as it has been for me. For I have at once revised plans for a training of trainers workshop, recognizing as never before the importance of consultations in advance, and of evolving the content of the workshop together with the participants, even though this will mean delay and extra costs.

This is more than just a guide to participatory curriculum development. It brings together a state-of-the-art collection of ideas, experience and methods for preparing, conducting, evaluating and following up on participatory courses and workshops. For anyone who wants to know about participatory curriculum development it must be an essential source. It is also a rich mine of practical ideas on training needs assessment, stakeholder analysis, the conduct of workshops, and much else.

This is a book whose time has come. It is accessible and authoritative, draws on practical theory, and based on experience and backed with case examples. To all who struggle to help others learn, I commend it. For myself, it will be an enduring source of ideas and inspiration.

Source: Taylor, P. (2003) *How to Design a Training Course: A guide to participatory curriculum development*. London: Continuum.

Reflections from Peter Taylor

> Peter Taylor is Director of Research at IDS. He spent 10 years at IDRC, Canada, as Director, Strategic Development, and as Director of the Think Tank Initiative. Over the last 30 years he has engaged frequently with Robert Chambers; at IDS as Leader of the Participation, Power and Social Change Team; as Education Technical Advisor with Helvetas in Vietnam; and as

> *Lecturer in Agricultural Education at AERDD, University of Reading. With a PhD and MSc in agricultural education, Peter has interests in the theory and practice of organizational learning and development, evaluation, and facilitation of participatory and social change processes.*

In 1991 I returned from four years working as a teacher of agriculture in a rural secondary school in Botswana, which was a lifechanging experience. I probably learned more from them than they learned from me, because they brought deep experience and knowledge about growing food in the most challenging ecological and climatic conditions. I quickly realized that everyone's learning experience would be enriched if everyone contributed actively to the learning process. This was quite a different approach from that which I had encountered as a trainee teacher in Scotland. I went back to the UK to study for a Master's in agricultural education and developed, with the adult educator Alan Rogers, an approach we termed 'participatory curriculum development'. We wrote a book about it for the FAO, and then over several years I had a chance to road test and ground truth in Africa and Asia the ideas and practices we had established as a starting point for others to try out, complement, and improve. I gained experience in many countries, and Vietnam provided particularly fertile ground for the approach, where I worked for almost a decade with forestry educators in universities and provincial rural extension services.

On return to Ireland from Vietnam after almost four years with the Swiss NGO Helvetas, I felt it would be worthwhile writing a book which explained the core ideas of participatory curriculum development and would offer practical ideas and suggestions for anyone interested in using this approach to design training courses. I developed the publication for VSO Books (as was), sourced a lovely set of illustrations from an artist friend in Hanoi, and asked Robert Chambers, who I had by then encountered in several interesting places and whose work I admired immensely, if he would be willing to write a foreword. True to form, he accepted the invitation with alacrity. It's sad that this is one foreword which didn't make it into the actual book, as the publisher and book changed hands, and somewhere this piece of the puzzle was lost in the transition. But it is wonderful to see it reappear now, albeit belatedly, in this excellent volume.

Reading his foreword again, it's not surprising that Robert provides words of encouragement and support to the author, to the users, and to everyone who is likely to benefit from the approach. He also sets out his own, powerfully held beliefs from the start: 'Formal and informal teaching, training and learning are human universals, vital for empowerment and a good life; and good education is considered a human right.' He emphasizes why education becomes more effective when it is grounded in participation and consultation. And he ends with the words: 'To all who struggle to help others learn, I commend it. For myself, it will be an enduring source of ideas and inspiration.' Robert has been an enduring source of ideas and inspiration to me as well and continues thus. I am sure he will, too, for so many others. Thank you, Robert.

Foreword to *The Ripped Chest* (2004) by Harsh Mander

> Harsh Mander is a prolific writer, researcher, and activist. Robert wrote the forewords to two of his books Unheard Voices: Stories of forgotten lives (*2001*) and The Ripped Chest (*2003*). The second of these is reproduced here, followed by a reflection from Harsh Mander himself.

It is a daunting honour to be invited to write a foreword for this book of Harsh Mander's. His earlier work, *Unheard Voices: Stories of forgotten lives*, is the most stark and disturbing description of the bad life of those who are poor and marginalised that I have ever read, and perhaps that has ever been written. It recounts the lives of poor people as they have told them. No reader can remain unmoved. Few can fail to feel outrage. For without pretension, it presents realities about the human condition which shame us all who are not poor and for which we all bear responsibility, but which I, and I dare say many readers, prefer to deny or shut out.

It is from that book that the title of this one is taken. A ripped chest is a cruel image of mutilation and pain. It links the forgotten lives of *Unheard Voices* and the world of public policy with which this book deals. Each book presents realities essential to the other. They should not be separated. I urge that they be read together. The first describes the unseen anguish, humiliation and deprivation typical of so many millions of lives. This second book now shows where so much of the responsibility lies, both in the machinery and servants of the state, and by implication with all of us who to varying degrees and in varied ways have power to make a difference.

We have here a work of magisterial range and scholarship. A book like this might have covered any one of the major groups of those who suffer poverty, discrimination and marginalisation. It could have been devoted either to the rural poor, or slum-dwellers and the homeless, or tribal people, or *dalits*, or oustees from dams and other projects. Instead it covers them all, and with convincing detail. To this is added the credibility and authority of one who speaks from hard-won experience in Government administration, and who has the scholarly commitment and personal courage to write about things as they are.

The shortcomings of Government policies and programmes designed to help and "uplift" the poor have been exposed before. What is new here is the cumulative effect of authoritative evidence from such a wide range of programmes and conditions. On the negative side, the abuses of human rights by a democratic state which are recounted are so distressing and so pervasive that it is difficult to understand how they can persist; and the combination of scale and ineffectiveness of some of the Government programmes described is little short of awesome. More than perhaps any other country, India has persevered with programmes targeted to individuals or households. So often, it seems, these either miss their targets or hit them and do more harm than good. The evidence is here that, however benign the intentions, what happens on the ground is often perverse, leaving poor people not empowered and prospering but weaker and poorer than before. There are exceptions, like self-targeting employment guarantee schemes. But overall the state and its servants appear as much problem as solution. Whether it is the misappropriations of top-down targeted rural programmes, the mindless oppression of petty urban traders by officials and of the homeless by police, the expropriation of their heritage and birthrights from tribal people, the dismal record of implementation of protective legislation for *dalits*, or the inhumanity with which so many dam oustees have been treated, it is not just the awfulness and injustice, but the sheer scale that is mind-blowing. To take just one example, the estimate that since 1947 some 50 million people may have been displaced by projects is but one illustration of the enormity of impoverishment inflicted in the name of development.

Despite all this evidence, the thrust is that of the positive practitioner who looks for what works and what can be done, not the negative academic who finds everything wrong and ends in impotence and despair. The new directions of hope of people's empowerment in Part III recognises the many difficulties and imperfections of the panchayati raj decentralisation and the obstacles of corruption. But it finds two sources of hope.

The first is leadership and human nature. His own experience and that of others who have attempted to fight corruption frontally has been that

> *"If strict and fair action against corruption is accompanied by motivation of staff, recognition of good work, and responsiveness to genuine grievances, employee motivation is found not to decline but in fact greatly blossom among the large majority of staff. Human nature is not by and large irredeemable."*

The second source of hope, powerfully argued by Mander, is rights to information. Transparency associated with people's planning in Kerala, and the movements for social audit and access to information in Rajasthan, are persuasive evidence that freedom of access to information is a key, if not the main key, to better governance. And the action needed is unequivocal.

Unheard Voices and *The Ripped Chest* are appeals for imagination, realism, solidarity, commitment, and action: for imagination and realism to recognise how the state so often promotes and perpetuates the persecution of the poor; for solidarity with them and commitment to change; and for resolute and sustained action to reform the policies of the state and the practices carried out in its name. The challenges are framed in India; but their span is global. There are lessons here for all of us, from whatever country or continent. Reflecting on these two books, the question is whether we, the readers, can match the tenacity and resilience of the many millions of the excluded and deprived who cannot and will not read them. It is whether we and those near to us can muster and sustain the courage to see and stand out for what is right.

Let me hope that *The Ripped Chest* will be widely available, widely read, and widely consulted. May it, together with *Unheard Voices*, provoke outrage and inspire action by the many who are in positions where they can make a difference. Most obviously and directly these are officials and politicians, at all levels, high, low and in the middle ranges. They are also the many in civil society – in NGOs, in the professions, in business, in unions – who are or can become in many different ways activists for change. And for all of these it is also their families who either undermine or support them in taking stands of courage and sacrifice. All have their part to play. For it is the accumulation of individual actions that counts. Some are dramatic and visible. Many appear mundane and are seen by only a few. All matter. All can make a difference. All can combine and contribute to movements. May *The Ripped Chest* inform and encourage that brave vanguard of Government officers and activists who already confront secrecy, corruption and malpractice and who are already committed to transparency, honesty and justice. May it also encourage many others to join them. For there is nothing inevitable about the bad life experienced each day by so many crores of poor and marginalised people. That bad life is made by us, by humankind. And what we make we can unmake. *The Ripped Chest* shows us many ways in which this has to be done. May it inspire good actions and much change for the better.

Source: Mander, H. (2004) *The Ripped Chest: Public policy and the poor in India*. Bangalore: Books for Change.

Reflections from Harsh Mander

> *Harsh Mander, human rights and peace worker, writer, columnist, researcher, and teacher, works with survivors of mass violence, hunger, homeless persons, and street children. He is Chairperson, Centre for Equity Studies, devoted to analysis*

and development of public policy and law for justice and rights of disadvantaged groups. He convenes and edits the annual India Exclusion Report. In all of this, he has often reached out to Robert, who has in all times been both generous and wise with his insights. A prolific writer, his 25 books include two for which Robert wrote the foreword: Unheard Voices: Stories of forgotten lives *(Penguin, India, 2001) and* The Ripped Chest *(Books for Change, 2004). For his PhD from Vrije University in Amsterdam, Robert was part of his viva committee. His thesis was titled* Vulnerable People and Policy Development in India: Designing State Interventions for Hunger, Homelessness, Destitution and Targeted Violence. *To counter rising hate violence and lynching, he leads the national initiative called the Karwan e Mohabbat or Caravan of Love, for atonement, solidarity, healing, conscience, and justice.*

Robert Chambers wrote generous, thoughtful, and penetrating forewords for two of my early books, *Unheard Voices: Stories of forgotten lives* (Penguin India, 2001) and *The Ripped Chest: Public Policy and the Poor* (Books for Change, 2004).

I know few people who have contributed more to decolonizing and democratizing knowledge creation and social science research than Robert Chambers. His path-breaking derives from his genuine and profound respect for the wisdom and insight of working people who may have not had the opportunities of formal education. He has taught two generations of researchers and activists by his writings as much as his praxis, curiosity, and ways of attentive listening and reflection with people he recognized to be the real 'experts' of poverty, namely people who live in poverty.

For a person of such formidable intellect combined with a deep humanism to agree to write the forewords to my two early books (and blurbs for others that followed) was a great privilege.

In the first book *Unheard Voices* I tried to write real-life stories of a range of people who lived with various forms of discrimination and dispossession – including survivors of religious, caste, and gender violence, of stigmatized ailments like leprosy and HIV, of industrial disasters like the Bhopal Gas leakage, and natural disasters like the Odisha super-cyclone; of displacement by mega-dams; sex workers and homeless people, and many others. The second book *The Ripped Chest* attempted to apply a microscope to public policy, law, and programmes to identify forensically in which precise ways they have failed the poor.

When I read and reread his forewords to my books, I am struck each time by his rare generosity of both heart and intellect. Unlike many people of his standing and reputation, he does not simply lend his name to a book by another writer. His generosity is much deeper. He clearly has given each book his very careful attention, and when he talks about the books, he overlooks their undoubted flaws, and instead highlights, even celebrates what he sees as their strengths, what he learns from the books. This reflects his genuine humility, his openness to always learning anew, from each of those who cross his path.

I am therefore delighted that an anthology is being collected of various prefaces and forewords that Robert Chambers wrote over many decades. Read together, these will offer a masterclass in towering intellect, which is always humble, curious, attentive, generous, and humane.

Foreword to *Exploring the Science of Complexity: Ideas and implications for development and humanitarian efforts* (2008) by Ben Ramalingam and Harry Jones with Toussaint Reba and John Young

> *This is Robert's foreword to an ODI (Overseas Development Institute) working paper. The inclusion of a foreword in a working paper is somewhat unconventional, but Ben Ramalingam recognized the value it would add, and was aware of Robert's interest in systems thinking. Robert's foreword is followed by a contribution from Marina Apgar, who is working with some of the ideas in this paper within the field of research evaluation.*

Much development and humanitarian thinking and practice is still trapped in a paradigm of predictable linear causality and maintained by mindsets that seek accountability through top-down command and control. Recent years have seen more emphasis on the mechanistic approaches of this paradigm and kinds of procedures long since abandoned by successful private sector organisations.

This has widened the gap between actual aid practices and the rhetoric of the many initiatives which aim to improve them – including aid effectiveness, institutional reform, participation, local ownership and empowerment.

In the meantime in parallel, complexity science has explored and articulated a contrasting world of understanding, helping to explain complex dynamic phenomena in a widely diverse range of settings with insights and concepts like non-linearity, edge of chaos, self-organisation, emergence and co-evolution.

This Working Paper is, to my knowledge, the first comprehensive and substantial work to be published that attempts, systematically and thoroughly, to bridge these two worlds, explaining and then relating the ideas of contemporary complexity theory to current development and humanitarian thinking and practice. Ten concepts of complexity science are articulated and provide us with lenses through which to examine, and see differently, the realities with which we grapple in international aid work.[1]

Ben Ramalingam and his colleagues describe and interpret a world of messy and unpredictable change which corresponds with much experience in the aid sector. They challenge dominant ideas and practices of development and change, locked in as these are to linear thinking and to procedures and requirements such as the logical framework and impact assessments. With scholarly authority and illustration, they explore the implications for how we see and think about development and humanitarian work. In doing so, they help to make clearer why so much aid is so problematic, in both conception and execution.

Exploring the Science of Complexity should provoke and inspire changes in aid thinking and practice that will lead to greater realism. Realism means more modesty and more honesty, which will not be easy. The authors suggest that political, professional, institutional and personal changes are necessary. Such changes require transformations of power relations, procedures, mindsets, behaviours, and professional education and training. More than anything, these changes demand the exercise of agency by individuals with the vision, commitment and courage to learn from and champion new and challenging approaches.

Let me hope that the ideas and orientations explored here will be understood and internalised by policy-makers and others with power, as well as by researchers, analysts and managers; that this will lead to norms, actions and relationships that will make development and humanitarian practice more attuned to reality, more sensitive to context, more adaptive, less reductionist and less simplistic; and that this will in turn generate and enable changes that enhance social justice and are more effectively pro-poor.

The potential is there. The need is there. We have in this Working Paper new analysis and insights to inform, inspire and underpin the radical changes in mindsets and practice required. It is now up to readers to read, reflect, debate, internalise and use these insights to find new and creative ways to bring about a better world.

Source: Ramalingam, B. and Jones, H. with Reba, T. and Young, J. (2008) *Exploring the Science of Complexity: Ideas and implications for development and humanitarian efforts*, 2nd edition. London: Overseas Development Institute. Reproduced by permission.

Note

1. The ten concepts of complexity science elaborated in the text are:

Complexity and systems:

- *Interconnected and interdependent elements and dimensions*
- *Feedback processes promote and inhibit change within systems*
- *System characteristics and behaviours emerge from simple rules and interactions*

Complexity and change:

- *Non-linearity*
- *Sensitivity to initial conditions*
- *Phase space – the 'space of the possible'*
- *Attractors, chaos and the 'edge of chaos'*

Complexity and agency:

- *Adaptive agents*
- *Self-organization*
- *Co-evolution*

Reflections from Marina Apgar

Marina Apgar is Research Fellow in the Participation, Inclusion and Social Change cluster at IDS. She has over 20 years' experience in exploring and building an evidence base for participatory methodologies and programming in response to complex challenges with marginalized people. Marina has collaborated with Robert Chambers, Ben Ramalingam, and many others to support practical and conceptual advances in the practice of complexity-aware and adaptive programming, in particular through her expertise in participatory and systemic evaluation.

In 2008, when Ben Ramalingam and colleagues produced the first substantive attempt to situate what complexity could mean to the development and humanitarian sectors in an ODI working paper, they were challenging dominant ideas of linear and top-down aid. Robert Chambers himself had been challenging these same ideas for some time, arguing that the unpredictability of development which arises when it is viewed through the lens of complexity, suggests that diverse, locally grounded responses should be nurtured instead of imposing top-down and externally designed solutions (Chambers, 1997). In some circles, in particular those advocating for 'people focused development' these ideas were not controversial, because of our natural affinity with seeing the world as messy and unpredictable, an emic view, embodied in people's lived experience. In other circles, however, the fit is not so comfortable.

In my own experience in the context of evaluation research, the dominance of paradigms (and methods they are fused with) that can answer the 'what works' question to neatly measure the effectiveness of predefined and planned interventions is one of the hardest to shift. And perhaps is one of the most important ones to focus on, given that evidence shapes funding decisions and has a wide impact on all aspects of development. Yet, even in the narrow and politically challenging context of evaluation, we are experiencing a shift towards broadening of possible designs that evaluators can choose from. We are moving away from methodological dogma, to meet the demands of programmes, and become methodological pluralists. The sector is increasingly focusing on responding to 'intractable' development challenges in the context of intersecting crises. And in some (more progressive) pockets of aid and in particular philanthropy, supporting social justice for those historically marginalized and often racialized communities is also gaining traction. In such conditions of complexity – where development is not simply a technical endeavour and requires that we work across sectors and stakeholders – evaluation and programme design that is fit for purpose has to work with unpredictable causal pathways in new and creative ways. Robert Chambers, in 2015 put forward the notion of 'inclusive rigour' as a way to rethink rigour to work with rather than against complexity (Chambers, 2015). This, alongside other trends in evaluation practice and theory, has produced a wide range of 'complexity-aware' evaluation designs and methods to choose from, and within them a subset that help us deepen participation, navigate power, and support equity (Apgar and Allan, 2021).

And while we can celebrate how Ramalingam and colleagues inspired a move towards more complexity-aware development, and within this a participatory emphasis provided by Robert Chambers and echoed by other leading participatory methodologists (Burns and Worsley, 2015), the paradigm shift remains incomplete. In particular, the hope Robert Chambers expressed in his foreword that power relations will be transformed and new mindsets and behaviours will follow is still, very much work in progress. Indeed, as we see a conservative political shift in aid in some parts of the world, for all of us engaged in international development work, as critical scholars, as practitioners, as evaluators, and as decision makers, grappling with being true to the reality of messy, complex processes of change must remain a daily struggle.

References

Apgar, M. and Allen, W. (2021). 'Participatory monitoring evaluation and learning: taking stock and breaking new ground'. In The *SAGE Handbook of Participatory Research and Inquiry*, London: SAGE, pp. 829–935.

Burns, D. and Worsley, S. (2015). *Navigating Complexity in International Development: Facilitating sustainable change at scale*. Rugby: Practical Action Publishing.

Chambers, R. (1997). *Whose Reality Counts? Putting the last first*. London: ITDG Publishing.

Chambers, R. (2015). 'Inclusive rigour for complexity'. *Journal of Development Effectiveness* 7(3): 327–35. https://doi.org/10.1080/19439342.2015.1068356

Foreword to *Seasonality, Rural Livelihoods and Development* (2011) edited by Stephen Devereux, Robert Chambers, Rachel Sabates-Wheeler, and Richard Longhurst

> *Richard Longhurst (2011) describes Robert's early realizations in the 1970s about the importance of seasonality in the lives of the rural poor. He notes also, the extent to which urban dwellers, who tend to be those that design policies and programmes that aim to improve the lives of these rural poor, tend to be entirely blind to the effects of seasonality. Stephen Devereux writes here, that despite the decades of work on seasonality, it remains under-recognized, and often poorly understood. Hence the need for the* Seasonality Revisited *conference convened in 2009 at IDS, which led to this publication in 2011.*

As a dimension of poverty, seasonality is as glaringly obvious as it is still grossly neglected. Attempts to embed its recognition in professional mindsets, policy and practice have still a long way to go.

There is some history here. The discovery in a seminar at the Institute of Development Studies (IDS), University of Sussex in the mid-1970s that births peaked towards the ends of the rains both in rural Bangladesh and in northern Nigeria, raised intriguing questions and opened up the whole subject. Many seasonal deprivations and stresses were recognized to coincide during the tropical rains – hard work, lack of food, shortage of money and vulnerability to debt, sicknesses, isolation and lack of access to services and markets, among others. To explore and learn more about these and other dimensions, and how they interlinked, a conference was held at IDS in July 1978. This was convened jointly by Richard Longhurst and myself from IDS and David Bradley and Richard Feachem from the London School of Hygiene and Tropical Medicine. *Seasonal Dimensions to Rural Poverty* (Chambers et al., 1981) brought together the edited papers. These were contributions mainly from specialized professional perspectives with sections on climatic seasonality, energy relationships and food, economic relationships and the seasonal use of labour, the seasonal ecology of disease, patterns of births and death, family health and seasonal welfare, and the social distribution of seasonal burdens.

The overarching concerns were to see how these coincided and were connected, and to identify what might be done. We saw that the rains were when many people were poorest and most vulnerable to becoming poorer.

We hoped that once and for all *Seasonal Dimensions to Rural Poverty* would place seasonality firmly in the minds of professionals and on the agenda of policy and practice. The hope was in vain. Several books and an IDS Bulletin with seasonality as a theme were indeed published (Longhurst, 1986; Sahn, 1989; Chen, 1991; Gill, 1991; Ulijaszek and Strickland, 1993), but their impact was limited. Throughout the three decades since the 1978 conference seasonality remained largely a professional and policy blind spot. By 2008, however, work on food security and social protection was again placing seasonality on the agenda, notably through *Seasons of Hunger* (Devereux et al., 2008) with its insight that 'seasonal hunger is the father of famine'. It was time for another conference – to review changes, introduce new perspectives, propose actions, and more decisively and lastingly, if possible, to raise professional awareness and enhance policy relevance. The *Seasonality Revisited* conference was convened at the Institute of Development Studies in July 2009. The chapters that follow are edited from the papers presented.

The 1978 conference and book were strong on health and technical aspects of nutrition, and much of that still applies. With the second conference, old topics like migration were updated and new topics reflected changes that have taken place since – notably HIV and AIDS vulnerabilities and disabilities, policy interventions such as social protection, and innovations in monitoring livelihoods for enhanced understanding of seasonality. In the 2009 conference, social protection and food security moved centre stage. Neither of these terms was in use in 1978. But the most fundamental new topic is climate change affecting seasons, threatening radical changes for agriculture and possibly almost everything else.

Changes since 1978

Generalizations about adverse seasonality have always been open to exceptions. As recognized in 1978, conditions and experiences of seasonality vary by location, occupation, gender, wealth and poverty, age, caste and class, and control of resources. Further, generalizations seem more difficult now than they were in 1978. There have been major demographic changes, not least in increasing urbanization and the rising numbers of poor people in urban areas. But in its many varied forms, seasonality for poor people – urban or rural, farmers, labourers or in other occupations – remains both significant and neglected.

Significant trends and changes have affected adverse seasonalities since the 1970s. On the positive side, access to markets and health services has improved in many countries. Seasonal isolation is still prevalent but has diminished: networks of all-weather roads in many countries penetrate further into rural hinterlands. Mobile phones have dramatically improved communications with many innovations:

M-Pesa in Kenya and neighbouring countries, for instance, enables instant transfers of money even to 'remote' areas. Where people are now less poor, so they are less vulnerable to seasonal stresses. Counter-seasonal and relief programmes for poorer and more marginalized people, and social protection more broadly, have improved, transformed and spread, as evident in this book – not least the employment guarantee schemes of India, now spreading to other countries. Immunization programmes have achieved wider coverage. Polio and Guinea Worm Disease, the latter so devastating to communities precisely when they need to cultivate, have been eliminated or nearly eliminated in most of the world. Malaria, for all that it remains a scourge, has sharply declined in the East African coast.[1] And when stresses and shocks are so interlinked, the weakening or elimination of any one can diminish vulnerability to others and enhance resilience.

All the same, much has not changed. Seasonal shortages, stress and price scissors still screw poor rural people down in poverty, and shocks of accidents and illness have sudden downward ratchet effects from which people may not recover. In rural areas during tropical rainy seasons, many of the adverse factors continue to interlock: hard work, sickness, lack of food, poverty of time and energy, shortage of money, isolation and lack of access to markets and services still combine to make these times of multiple stresses and vulnerability for poor people.

Other conditions for poor rural people have worsened. Structural adjustment in many countries reduced rural access to education and health services, and led to a decline in maintenance of roads. Liberalization policies imposed on African countries reduced or eliminated subsidies and uniform pricing regimes. These had supported farmers and rural people throughout the year and had moderated adverse seasonal price scissor effects for selling crops and purchasing food. Liberalization in one country made it unviable for its neighbours to maintain subsidies and price supports because of cross-border leakage. Though these trends have been partially reversed, for example in Malawi, they still generally prevail. In many parts of Africa, a seasonal increase in theft is reported. Climate change has already had an impact, not just through warming, but also as shown in this book through rainy seasons becoming less reliable in their onset and end, and by bringing more intense rainfall at wider intervals. The long-term implications of these trends for agricultural livelihoods, especially in the semi-arid tropics, are serious. Even with adaptations of farming and cropping systems, they will make agriculture more risky and less viable for many, and are liable to reduce the production of food and non-food crops. For climatic seasonal effects on other dimensions of seasonality like disease, the patterns will be varied and are not always easy to foresee.

For the future

Past neglect means present and future potential. In 2011 we are in a stronger position to exploit that potential than we were in 1978. Three points stand out to put seasonality higher on the agenda and keep it there. The first is better recognition that it can be more cost-effective as well as more humane to use counter-seasonal measures to prevent poor people becoming poorer, rather than trying to help them struggle back up again once they have become poorer. But more research needs to be done to identify those measures that are most effective, and most cost-effective.

The second is social protection. There is now much discussion of counter-seasonal programmes (Hauenstein Swan et al., 2009) such as price-indexed cash transfers and seasonal employment programmes. Social protection as a concept can also be extended to transport infrastructure, access to markets, and livelihoods. Given the seasonality of sickness and the frequency with which seasonal sickness makes poor people poorer, effective, accessible and affordable health services can be recognized for what they are – a critical form of social protection.

The third, paradoxically, is climate change and its meteoric rise as a concern and priority. The links between climate change, seasonal disruption and agriculture can serve to draw attention to related seasonal vulnerabilities like sickness, hunger, isolation, stress and becoming poorer.

So this book is a standing invitation to development professionals, policymakers and academics. It is an invitation to enhance the relevance of their work to the reduction of poverty and illbeing. It is an invitation to explore seasonal dimensions in many disciplines, domains and specializations. It is an invitation to share the excitement of aha! moments on discovering how different dimensions interlink.

Seasonality, like sustainable livelihoods, is a common ground for many disciplines. It can sharpen the relevance of research and action. Poor rural people who experience negative and positive seasonalities know a great deal about them. Those of us who are neither rural nor poor have much to learn. Let me hope that many will be inspired by these pages to be sensitive to seasonal realities and join in the learning, and to see things and do things differently. May seasonality never again be so overlooked. And may this book inform and inspire many to work to banish avoidable seasonal suffering and poverty from our world.

Robert Chambers
2 April 2011

Note

1. The incidence of malaria in Kilifi District on the Kenya coast has dropped to one fifth of its level five or six years ago and there have been declines all along the East African coast (conversation at the Kenya Medical Research Institute, Kilifi, February 2009).

References

Chambers, R., Longhurst, R. and Pacey, A. (eds) (1981). *Seasonal Dimensions to Rural Poverty*. London: Frances Pinter.

Chen, M.A. (1991). *Coping with Seasonality and Drought*. New Delhi: Sage Publications.

Devereux, S., Vaitla, B. and Hauenstein Swan, S. (2008). *Seasons of Hunger*. London: Pluto Press.

Gill, G. (1991). *Seasonality and Agriculture in the Developing World: A problem of the poor and powerless*. Cambridge: Cambridge University Press.

Hauenstein Swan, S., Vaitla, B. and Devereux, S. (2009). 'An integrated intervention framework for fighting seasonal hunger', paper presented at the international conference, *Seasonality Revisited, 8–10 July, Institute of Development Studies, Brighton*.

Longhurst, R. (ed.) (1986). 'Seasonality and poverty', *IDS Bulletin*, vol 17, no 3. Brighton: Institute of Development Studies.

Longhurst, R. (2011). 'Seasonality: Uncovering the obvious and implementing the complex'. In Cornwall, A. and Scoones, I. (eds), *Revolutionizing Development: Reflections on the work of Robert Chambers*. London: Earthscan, pp. 101-106.

Sahn, D. (1989). *Seasonal Variability in Third World Agriculture: The consequences for food security*. Baltimore, MD: Johns Hopkins University Press.

Ulijaszek, S. and Strickland, S. (eds) (1993). *Seasonality and Human Ecology*. Cambridge: Cambridge University Press.

Source: Devereux, S., Sabates-Wheeler, R. and Longhurst, R. (eds.) (2011) *Seasonality, Rural Livelihoods and Development*. London: Routledge. Reproduced by permission of Taylor & Francis Group.

Reflections from Stephen Devereux

> Stephen Devereux is a Research Fellow at the UK Institute of Development Studies whose work focuses on food security and social protection. He developed a particular interest in seasonality after reading Seasonal Dimensions to Rural Poverty, co-edited by Robert Chambers, in the 1980s. He subsequently researched seasonal hunger in several African countries including Ethiopia, Ghana, Malawi, and South Africa.

Seasonal Dimensions to Rural Poverty (Chambers et al., 1981) shaped my career. I read this landmark book while planning my PhD fieldwork in the mid-1980s. I was struck by its insights into the adverse implications of seasonality in the tropics for many aspects of rural lives and livelihoods, and I decided to work on seasonal hunger in West Africa.

I wrote a research proposal to the UK's Overseas Development Administration that Robert kindly supported, titled 'Food security, seasonality and resource allocation in northeastern Ghana'. One morning two years later, when I woke up in a village in Upper East Region after the annual harvest, I could see the horizon for the first time. The dense fields of tall millet and sorghum had been cut to the ground. Cattle and goats that had been tethered for months during the cropping season were now roaming freely. The dry season in northern Ghana was like living in a different country.

Robert's brilliant satirical poem 'Ode to the Seasons Conference' that closes *Seasonal Dimensions to Rural Poverty* should be mandatory reading for all development students, activists, practitioners, and policy-makers. Statisticians, for instance: 'have a seasonal nightmare/An average is but a dream/With seasons means aren't what they seem'.

Three decades after *Seasonal Dimensions* was published in 1981, I was honoured to work with Robert, Rachel Sabates-Wheeler, and Richard Longhurst on a conference called *Seasonality Revisited* at IDS. We aimed to revive academic and policy interest in the topic by drawing attention to new drivers of adverse seasonality, notably economic liberalization and climate change. Robert participated with his usual inspiring enthusiasm and passion. He also contributed a chapter on seasonal interlinkages and integrated seasonal poverty, as well as the foreword, to the book of the conference.

Despite the pioneering work of Robert, his colleagues, and successors, seasonality remains a feature of life in the tropics that is under-recognized, poorly understood, and inadequately addressed by policy and programming. One reason was identified by Robert at the *Seasonality Revisited* conference: urban-based development professionals from Europe and North America remain 'season-proofed and season-blind' (Chambers, 2012).

But Robert is always optimistic. The day after our conference, he emailed the organizing team to express his appreciation: 'As a Rip Van Winkle lurker it was thrilling to be lured out of the woodwork and blink with wonder at what you had brought about, what was written, and what discussed and shared. May the follow up make a big difference. It is there waiting to be made!'

References

Chambers, R. (2012). 'Seasonal poverty: integrated, overlooked and therefore opportunity'. In S. Devereux, R. Longhurst and R. Sabates-Wheeler (eds), *Seasonality, Rural Livelihoods and Development*, p. 85. Abingdon: Earthscan.

Chambers, R., Longhurst, R., and Pacey, A. (eds) (1981). *Seasonal Dimensions to Rural Poverty*. London: Frances Pinter.

Afterword in *Who Counts?* (2013) edited by Jeremy Holland

> *I distinctly remember when Jeremy was working on this book because Robert, characteristically, was beside himself with excitement about it, and stopped me (and, no doubt, others) several times in the corridor to ask if I'd spoken to Jeremy, and if I'd heard about the amazing work he was doing with participatory statistics.*

This book presents evidence of a methodological breakthrough. This has for too long been unrecognized. Since 1991, when ActionAid Nepal facilitated a mapping study in over 130 villages to find out how many people had received services, the evidence has been there, and has been diversifying and accumulating, that participatory methods can generate excellent statistics. There has been a quiet methodological revolution. Great opportunities and potentials have been revealed. But the mainstreams of research, monitoring, and evaluation have been almost totally untouched.

Far from adopting participatory statistics, the direction of funding and fashion has sponsored and favoured a wider application of conventional methods for statistics and evidence in development. This book challenges such methodological conservatism and the direction it is taking. It shows that for many contexts and purposes there are alternatives which are more pro-poor, more accurate, more insightful, and more cost-effective, and that these, as Jeremy Holland points out in the introduction, are 'win–win': they can generate better statistics closer to ground realities to inform, influence, and improve policy and practice; and they can empower local people through their own analysis, learning, and data for use in action and advocacy.

Much has been learnt. Statistics generated through participatory processes can be and have been subject to the same tests as any other statistics (Barahona and Levy, 2003, 2007; Catley et al., 2008). They can be presented in tables just like any other numbers. They can be used for new indices: in 1996, in Bangladesh, a composite Prioritized Problem Index of Poor Communities was constructed for rural women, rural men, urban women, and urban men from problem rankings in 159 focus groups (UNDP 1996); and more recently, also in Bangladesh, a Group Development Index has been based on indicators assessed by thousands of groups (Jupp with Ibn Ali).

Beyond such normal approaches and uses of statistics, there are important differences and new insights.

'They can do it'

With good facilitation, often light and almost hands-off, local people have been found to have a far greater ability to model, map, assess, and quantify than most professionals have supposed. There are many illustrations in this book, for instance the participatory 3-dimensional modelling done by close to 120 villagers in Oromiya, Ethiopia (Rambaldi), the morbidity and mortality maps made by health field workers in the Philippines (Nierras), participatory indicator identification with farmers in Malawi (Cromwell et al.), group self-assessments of performance against 132 indicators by members of a social movement in Bangladesh (Jupp with Ibn Ali), and participatory impact assessments by farmers (Neubert), groups (Causemann et al.), and pastoralists (Abebe and Catley).

Methodological diversity and versatility

It is striking how diverse and versatile the approaches and methods are. Statistics can be generated in many ways for many purposes. We have mapping and modelling (Rambaldi, Shah). In Malawi, through a process including community mapping with cards, a table could be compiled showing food security status against the receipt of a government programme (Barahona). Aggregation from focus groups is well represented (Jupp; Moser and Stein; Neubert; Causemann et al.; Shah). In a participatory mode, almost anything that is qualitative, valued, and open to comparisons can be quantified, such as changes in empowerment and capabilities (Jupp and Ibn Ali); attitude and knowledge skills (Causemann et al.: 116); the importance of institutions (Moser and Stein); 'quality of life' (Neubert); poverty and wealth (Causemann et al.); wealth ranking into six standard categories at scale in the whole of rural Rwanda (Shah); trends in sustainability indicators (Cromwell et al.); and scoring satisfaction with services (Riemenschneider et al.). Versatility extends beyond census and service counting to, for instance, estimating changes in gender relations over a decade (MYRADA in Chambers, 1997: 174), or through matrices attributing effects or impacts to causes (Neubert; Catley et al., 2008). Indicators are again and again identified in a participatory mode, as in Bangladesh through listening study techniques, PRA methods, and participatory drama (Jupp), and in Malawi through extended interactive processes (Cromwell et al.), in both cases leading to many more indicators, of greater relevance, than would otherwise have been thought of. Diversity and versatility are evolutionary and adaptive, as Riemenschneider shows, with how what started as a longitudinal impact assessment becoming interactive research. Participatory approaches and methods can also generate statistics on hidden and sensitive subjects: as Shah points out concerning wealth and poverty, the Ubudehe maps in Rwanda make the invisible poor visible; and as others have shown, sensitive realities can be represented as with violence (Moser and McIlwaine, 2004), volumes of shit produced by a community (Kar, 2005), and teenage sexual behaviour and partner characteristics and preferences (Shah et al., 1999).

Participatory statistics tend to be more accurate than those from conventional methods

Accuracy comes from triangulation, cross-checking and processes of successive approximation. When participating analysts have overlapping knowledge of all the people in a community, there is little reason why any error should creep into a census: all participants can see and correct what is being shown. One common form of triangulation with tangible visualizations such as social mapping, matrix scoring, and pile sorting, is group-visual synergy,[1] where the facilitator can observe members of a group acting and interacting to converge successively on an agreed estimate or representation. Coverage of all project beneficiaries makes the NGO-IDEAS toolbox more rigorous than many research methods (Causemann et al.). Generally, rigour comes from relevance to the group, their overlapping knowledge and values, and their energy and commitment to 'trying to get it right'. These can be observed by the facilitator and assessed critically. Triangulation can also be between different groups and methods.[2]

Win–Win

As Jeremy Holland points out in his introduction, participatory statistics are a 'win–win': they are credible, often illuminate aspects that would otherwise be missed, and at the same time empower and enlighten participants. All learn together in the processes. Surprise insights can be valuable to all concerned and have policy implications. When participants in the Philippines workshop compared the maps they had made, they saw that the transition from communicable to degenerative diseases was beginning to manifest and that road accidents were the third most frequent cause of death (Nierras). Farmers in Malawi showed that they did not value the agroforestry that professionals believed to be a priority for them (Cromwell et al.). In the Maldives, researchers were taken aback by how much the methods were welcomed by key informants and how all gained from the feedback of findings (Riemenschneider et al.). Participatory well-being ranking can also identify those who are vulnerable and involve the rural rich in taking responsibility for the rural poor (Causemann et al.). P3DM in Ethiopia created a learning environment, and the elders who took part came to see more clearly the ecological changes that had taken place; and mapping brings peer-to-peer interactions and diagnostic analysis (Rambaldi). Knowledge embodied in the maps in Rwanda was democratized and made visible (Shah). Local governments in the Philippines became more responsive (Nierras) and downward accountability resulted in Bangladesh (Jupp). People found it empowering to become more aware of the effects of their actions (Causemann et al.). Consistently through all these examples, good statistics informed outsiders and empowered local participants.

Participatory statistics can have applications at the national level. In Rwanda, social maps offer a real-time census of populations in villages that can be and often are updated regularly by the communities themselves; and the Ministry of Health has used the maps for targeting households for free services and identifying who should be contributing to health insurance, and has invested in a data processing centre to capture and aggregate data from the maps more systematically (Shah). National statistics can be calibrated and corrected: in Malawi, participatory mapping in 54 carefully selected communities, cross-checked with a one-page household questionnaire, indicated a population 35 per cent higher than in the national census (Barahona and Levy, 2003, 2007). Discrepancies between national questionnaire surveys and participatory methods can raise questions of validity and credibility, as with the Uganda National Household Survey (Kagugube et al., 2009). All census studies and all household surveys might gain from such triangulation. In the Philippines workshops of health staff, statistics aggregated from midwives' records were found to be more accurate than those reported in the official data-gathering system, which they then replaced (Nierras). When health workers' statistics identified road accidents as the third cause of death, immediate action brought the death rate down. The 'robust, insightful and timely' statistical data from the participatory impact assessment of destocking in Ethiopia fed into key policy discussions and guidelines (Abebe and Catley).

Potentials

Many potentials are evident from what we have learnt. Given local people's capabilities and the versatility, accuracy, win–win character, and other advantages of participatory statistics, future adaptation, innovations, and applications promise to be innumerable. The power and sophistication of visual and tactile analysis with group-visual synergies in a PRA mode is an abiding strength, and has many applications. In addition, we now have ICTs and digital technologies. These open up unbounded new fields. Geospatial information technologies can express and assert local knowledge and rights (Rambaldi). Ultra-mobile personal computers bring opportunities for rapid analysis, feedback, and triangulation of participatory data (Riemenschneider et al.). Mobile phones, SMS, and crowdsourcing add to the proliferation of participatory methods and methodologies, raising new questions of inclusion, exclusion, representativeness, and data quality.

National and local statistics are one frontier (Barahona and Levy, 2007). The use of cloth maps in each of the 14,837 villages in Rwanda as a source of national statistics for health (Shah) takes us far beyond anything that could have been conceived a few years ago, and points to opportunities with monitoring other sectors, and social and economic change, in Rwanda and other countries. Sarah Levy (2007), reflecting on her experience with participatory research in Malawi, has outlined a vision of locally managed resource centres that would generate statistics as tools for local decision making and advocacy, while also producing timely and accessible data for national and decentralized evidence-based policy-making. In sum, in research, monitoring, and evaluation, and for local and national statistics, there seems to be almost no limit to the frontiers that participatory statistics have opened up and which are now waiting to be explored and exploited.

Practical and professional blocks

The evidence in this book and elsewhere in the literature indicates, again and again, that if participatory statistics were more the norm, there would then be substantial gains all round. But examples that have been written up are not a mainland, but an archipelago, small and scattered islands in a vast ocean of business-as-usual. Anyone reading the cases in this book will recognize their win–win potential. Though the power of participatory statistics has been known for over two decades, they have not taken off to become widespread practice in research, in social development, or in national statistics. We have to ask what is stopping them. Three practical and professional blocks stand out and each can be confronted.

The first is paradigmatic, to do with rigour. Rigour has come to be associated with the canons of some scientific and medical research, especially randomized control trials. These belong in a reductionist Cartesian–Newtonian paradigm and can make sense in some standardized, relatively controlled and uniform conditions. For conditions of complexity, diversity, emergence, and unpredictability they are a bad fit. For these conditions, more timely, relevant, and credible learning can be sought through the rigour of a paradigm of adaptive pluralism.[3] But 'rigour' and 'rigorous' are embedded in many professional mindsets as referring only to the reductionist paradigm; other approaches have tended to be dismissed as anecdotal, soft, and unrigorous. Paradigms, mindsets, vocabulary, and often the power of funding reinforce methodological conservatism. But now we see that participatory statistics can span and transcend the paradigms by combining the (Cartesian–Newtonian) rigour of statistical methods with the (adaptive, pluralist) rigour of a close fit, with complex and emergent local realities. Through the good practices of both paradigms, they can be doubly rigorous, and promise the best of both worlds.

The second explanation is risk-aversion, routinization, and inertia. Participatory statistics are generated through innovation, often creatively and interactively evolved for context and purpose. This takes time and money. It may also be felt to be risky. It is seen as easier and safer to follow approaches and methods that are routinized and embodied in manuals and which are taught in education and training institutions, and with which field workers are familiar. Professionals in aid organizations have expressed enthusiasm for piloting participatory statistics, but no action has followed. This does not necessarily mean that they have not tried: it may mean that they have met objections. Anyone promoting participatory statistics can expect professional and bureaucratic resistance. Inertia and the path of least resistance mean more of the same. Caution and convenience combine in a compelling case for questionnaires. Promotion of participatory statistics needs convinced and courageous champions. But on their own they may not be able to succeed. They need colleagues who do not oppose them, but who actively provide support.

The third explanation is the shortage of creative facilitators and lack of efforts to record and spread their innovations and skills. Not many researchers, whether academic or based in research institutes, have the orientation, experience, or competence to innovate and pilot participatory methodologies or to train others in them. Outstanding exceptions are to be found in this volume. Two trainer champions in the Rwandan Government have been key to the roll-out of Ubudehe. Those with competence are often freelance consultants, but they are in short supply. Moreover, when they have completed their contracts, neither they nor their sponsors have interest or resources for writing up, let alone training others and disseminating a new methodology they have developed. Their innovations are then not an enduring legacy, but one-off and transient.

Ethics

Ethical issues with participatory statistics were recognized and explored in detail by a network in the early 2000s.[4] No succinct summary can do justice to the principles and prescriptions of the *Guidelines and a Code of Conduct* which the network collectively produced and which remains an important source. What follows should be read together with Barahona's chapter on ethical considerations in which they stress transparency, consent, and confidentiality.

The guidelines outline the principles of participatory research. They then describe ideals of good practice with participatory research designed to produce numbers. Many of these apply to most or all research, like not raising expectations, assuring consent, not assuming approval of personal exposure or willingness to share data, not exposing people to risks, respecting confidentiality, and being sensitive to power relations. Others are of particular relevance to good practice in the participatory numbers context:

- being transparent when introducing externally driven research questions and ensuring a locally approved research agenda;
- feeding back findings to communities and maximizing the impact of community-generated data on external audiences and doing these especially when a study has an extractive element, eliciting information for use elsewhere;
- empowering participants through their own data generation, analysis, action, and ownership;
- optimizing trade-offs between representativeness and empowerment and standardization and empowerment, and when they occur between external pressures for results and ethical ideals.

Inevitable trade-offs demand that practitioners are continuously aware and reflective, struggle to optimize, and are transparent about the compromises and trade-offs they are making. Care is needed to avoid either of two extremes: one, being driven by contracts, deadlines, and external demands to cut corners and, under pressure, exploit and expose local people; and the other, striving towards ideals and seeking to follow principles to a point of paralysis. The first is the greater danger. To achieve a balance, managing the tensions and optimizing the trade-offs inherent in participatory statistics work, requires resolution and commitment on the part of facilitators and researchers to ethical principles, and awareness and understanding on the part of those responsible for commissioning and funding.

Ways forward

To realize the potentials of participatory statistics requires transformative revolutions which are at once professional, institutional, and personal.

First, professionally, evidence of the rigour, win–win, and strengths and weaknesses of participatory statistics needs repeated analysis, articulation, and dissemination. Jupp records how there was a breakthrough in acceptance of the participatory processes and statistics of the Bangladesh social movement. It was when an expensive external evaluation corroborated the movement's own data. It was then that other donors began to accept the data. More such studies are needed, including on cost-effectiveness and trade-offs. In paradigmatic and practical terms, it has to be recognized that time, commitment, and flair are needed to develop, adapt, pilot, and refine methods. To develop the methodology for the Malawi sustainability study took a team three weeks of intensive hands-on participatory trials and innovations in the in-depth preliminary field study, leading to the production of a field facilitators' manual with the 15 standard indicators (Cromwell and Fiona Chambers, pers. comm.). Good professional practice for participatory statistics has to include time and space for developing methodology in the early stages as a condition for quality and speed later, and overall cost-effectiveness.

Second, institutionally, teaching and training curricula need to incorporate participatory statistics, and participatory approaches and methods more generally. For this to be effective, faculty have themselves to gain field experience. Again and again, hands-on fieldwork has proved vital for conviction and confidence. Breakthroughs into the mainstream can take various forms: an example is when the well-known textbook *Veterinary Epidemiology* (Thrusfield, 2005, cited in Catley, 2009) included a section on 'participatory epidemiology', a field in which participatory statistics were prominent. Institutionally, the transformation needed requires the widespread incorporation of the principles, practices, and range of applications of participatory statistics in tertiary education, in training institutes, in textbooks, and in courses, and involving students in real-life practicals.

The third, personal, dimension is universal and fundamental. The way in is always through people and agency. Innovation needs champions. It is individuals who can change professional norms and methods, who can introduce participatory statistics into contracts and into courses, and who can foster and provoke institutional change. It is creative facilitators who can invent and pilot approaches and methods to fit purpose and contexts of local diversity and complexity. It is creative champions and those who support them who will be the transformers. And it is more than innovation that is needed. In Dee Jupp's words (2007: 122), 'It is not innovation but innovativeness ... that needs to be nurtured'.

Such innovative champions are among the authors in this book. Some work in NGOs. Freelance consultants are well represented. A common pattern is for a creative innovator to become frustrated with the constraints of her[5] organization, and to take the plunge of leaving and launching out as an independent. Unlike embedded academics or trainers, such freelancers have a degree of freedom, depending on their assignments, to innovate. What they need is time and tolerance on the part of their sponsors, often in governments or donor agencies, so that they can develop and test methodologies – a process which, if done well, will take a matter of weeks. And then when implementation is complete, they need support to write up the experience for a wider audience, and sometimes to train others. But these before and after blocks of time are rare in contracts, or severely squeezed. It would be a significant breakthrough, with high payoffs, if it became the norm for those who sponsor innovation with participatory statistics to set aside resources and time for these activities: through time and capacity before application, to enhance the quality and local fit of innovations; and through time and capacity after it, to disseminate generalizable learning, approaches, and methods.

If participatory statistics are to fulfil anything like their potential, they need resolute, imaginative, and sustained support. The establishment of participatory statistics in livestock epidemiology in East Africa was the result of sensitivity to professional concerns, a decade of methodological innovation, field exposure of university faculty and government officials, and a track record of high-quality data (Catley, 2009). This is inspiring, but may be difficult to replicate without sustained external support. Unfortunately, such support tends to be short term. There is no organization in our world dedicated to developing and disseminating participatory statistics. This is a glaring gap and omission, and a testimony to conservatism, ignorance, and lack of imagination. It also reflects a failure on the part of those of us who have long been aware of the potentials. I am angry with myself for not having done more. I am frustrated at the failure of any organization to see the need and seize the opportunity. For a few years over a decade ago, the Statistical Services Centre at the University of Reading conducted annual 10-day courses in participatory statistics, but lack of demand brought them to a close. I hope that after this book such a closure could never happen again. One of the most pro-poor and cost-effective investments a funding agency could make now would be to sponsor and support a global knowledge and innovation hub for participatory statistics. Its activities would include commissioning innovators to document and share their experiences, training and mentoring creative facilitators, and networking and nurturing a worldwide community of practice.

In conclusion

After this book, there can be no more excuses of ignorance. Those who do not explore participatory statistics can plead lack of time, lack of resources, lack of creative and innovative facilitators, the power and conservatism of others, their own or others' reluctance to take risks, or their own lack of confidence in making the case, but they cannot plead ignorance. Let me hope that the evidence presented here will inform and energize teachers, trainers, researchers, officials, funders, and other professionals; that it will give them confidence and ammunition to use in making the case for participatory statistics; and that in consequence, much professionalism, teaching, training, and commissioning of research will not just change, but be transformed.

The vision can then be of a future in which many millions of those who are poor, marginalized, and excluded are empowered through what they learn through their own analysis and the statistics and maps they generate, and those in power are better informed and driven to action as a result. It is a future in which modes of research, monitoring, and evaluation are determined not by conventional routines, but by creative innovation. It is a future in which core academic and official perceptions are more up to date and in touch with grass-roots realities. It is a future of win–win, empowering poor people, and giving those with power more timely, accurate, and credible information and insights into rapidly changing realities. Let me hope that this book and its contributors will inspire many, many others to join them in the vanguard of pioneers to bring that future about.

Robert Chambers, 23 June 2012

Notes

1. For a fuller discussion of the rigour of group-visual synergy and of participatory methods and approaches, see Chambers, 1997: 158–61.
2. For a helpful discussion and diagram, see Catley et al., 2008: 57–8.
3. I have tried to elaborate the contrasting paradigms in Chambers, 2010.
4. The Parti-Numbers Network of Southern and Northern practitioners and academics was established by members of the Institute of Development Studies (University of Sussex), the Centre for Development Studies (University of Wales, Swansea), the Statistical Services Centre and Integrated Rural Development Department (University of Reading), the Overseas Development Institute, and the International HIV/AIDS Alliance. It was much concerned with ethics. This led to Guidelines and a Code of Conduct on which this brief section is based.
5. Empirically, most of them, at least those based in the UK, are women.

References

Barahona, C. and Levy, S. (2003) 'How to generate statistics and influence policy using participatory methods in research: reflections on work in Malawi 1999–2002', IDS Working Paper 212, Institute of Development Studies, Sussex, UK.

Barahona, C. and Levy, S. (2007) 'The best of both worlds: producing national statistics using participatory methods', *World Development* 35, 2: 326–41.

Catley, A. (2009) 'From Marginal to Normative: Institutionalizing Participatory Epidemiology', in I. Scoones and J. Thompson (eds), *Farmer First Revisited*, Rugby: Practical Action Publishing: 247–54

Catley, A., Burns, J., Abebe, D., and Suji, S. (2008) *Participatory Impact Assessment: A Guide for Practitioners*, Feinstein International Center, Tufts University, Medford, MA.

Chambers, R. (1997) *Whose Reality Counts? Putting the First Last*, Practical Action Publishing, Rugby, UK.
Chambers, R. (2010) 'Paradigms, poverty and adaptive pluralism', IDS Working Paper 344, IDS Brighton, UK.
Jupp, D. (2007) 'Keeping the art of participation bubbling: some reflections on what stimulates creativity in using participatory methods', in Pettit and Brock (eds), *Springs of Participation*, pp. 107–22.
Kagugube, J., Ssewakiryanga, R., Barahona, C., and Levy, S. (2009) 'Integrating qualitative dimensions of poverty into the Third Uganda National Household Survey' (UNHS III), *Journal of African Statistics* 8: 28–52.
Kar, K. (2005) *Practical Guide to Triggering Community-Led Total Sanitation*, IDS, Brighton.
Kar, K. with Chambers, R. (2008) *Handbook on Community-Led Total Sanitation*, IDS Sussex and Plan International, UK. Available from: www.communityledtotalsanitation.org
Levy, S. (2007) 'Using numerical data from participatory research to support the Millennium Development Goals: the case for locally owned information systems', in Brock and Pettit (eds), *Springs of Participation*, pp. 137–49.
Moser, C. and Holland, H. (1997) *Urban Poverty and Violence in Jamaica*, World Bank, Washington, DC.
Moser, C. and McIlwaine, C. (2004) *Encounters with Violence in Latin America: Urban Poor Perceptions from Colombia and Guatemala*, Routledge, New York and London.
Pettit, J. and Brock, K. (eds) (2007) *Springs of Participation: Creating and Evolving Methods for Participatory Development*, Practical Action Publishing, Rugby, UK.
Shah, M.K., Degnan Kambou, S. and Monahan, B. (eds) (1999) *Embracing Participation in Development: Worldwide Experience from CARE's Reproductive Health Programs with a Step-by-step Field Guide to Participatory Tools and Techniques*, CARE, Atlanta, GA.
Thrusfield, M. (2005) *Veterinary Epidemiology*, 3rd edn, Blackwell Science, Oxford.
United Nations Development Programme (UNDP), Bangladesh (1996) *UNDP's 1996 Report on Human Development in Bangladesh, Vol. 3, Poor People's Perspectives*, UNDP, Dhaka.

Source: Holland, J. (ed.) (2013). *Who Counts? The power of participatory statistics.* Rugby: Practical Action Publishing.

Reflections from Jeremy Holland

Who Counts? was the culmination of several years of collaborative work, inspired and driven by Robert, on the power of participatory statistics for transformative change. Years of experience and reverse learning had convinced Robert that numbers had a particular power when in the hands of the powerless and in the face of institutions that would conventionally control such data.

To this end, Robert purposefully reached out to quantitative practitioners, most wedded to the 'gold standard' of randomized control trials and 'brute data'. He engaged in mixed-method initiatives hosted by the World Bank and others, always willing to be humble in the face of institutional 'experts'. Robert realized that he needed allies and champions among applied researchers across the epistemological divide. He reached out to social statisticians who were sceptical of the conventions that were applied by the 'randomistas'. At the same time, he sought out champions among conventional anthropologists and ethnographers who for their part were sceptical of attempts to dilute 'interpretive depth' via the 'reductionist' tendencies of crude numbers and accompanying notions of absolute truth. In this way, he built an interdisciplinary 'participatory numbers' community of practice with clearly articulated shared values of locally led, inclusive, and transformative change.

The book *Who Counts?* was steered forward by this community of practice. It brought together 10 years or more of practical experience of working with participatory statistics in policy and programme settings. This community and its body of work excited Robert, surely proof positive that generating numbers from the bottom up was both intrinsically empowering for local people and had instrumental utility for outsiders? The emergence of virtual real-time and crowd-sourced data at this time only added to the sense of possibility for a democratization of data generation. Since the book's publication, the community has dispersed but continues its work, although without the transformation called for by Robert's rallying cry in *Who Counts?* Conventional big data still rules the roost in the development field. However, there have been encouraging trends in the 10 years since the book's publication. We have seen wider debates within global policy around localization and indigenization that reposition 'beneficiaries' as active subjects in their relationship with development practitioners. This has shifted the debate progressively in ways that allow for local knowledge and locally generated data to be privileged. At the same time new methods – such as mass storytelling tools with quantifiable signification questions – have evolved in ways that accelerate the bridging of the methodological gap within a participatory paradigm, generating quantitative data at scale for confidence of inference while facilitating local processes of transformative change. Onwards!

Foreword to *Poverty and Development in China: Alternative approaches to poverty assessment* (2013) by Caizhen Lu

> What this book does, according to Robert, better than any other, is show how different methodological approaches to measuring poverty yield entirely different results. Thus, the book offers not just rich insight into rural poverty in a particular context, but also a complex assessment of the different possible measurement tools. Robert's foreword does a far more comprehensive job of explaining this and is followed by a reflection piece by Tami Blumenfield, a scholar who is familiar with both Robert's work and Caizhen Lu's, and has worked extensively in rural China.

To be invited to write a foreword to a book as remarkable as *Poverty and Development in China* is a privilege and a challenge. For this book makes major original contributions to poverty research and to understanding how we understand and identify poverty. It gives rich and credible insights into life, conditions and poverty in rural China. Beyond that, it raises sharp questions with universal significance about methodology and policy. It illuminates the strengths and weaknesses of alternative methodologies. And it shows how our methods determine what we learn, who we consider to be poor and what we decide should be done. It confronts all of us who are concerned with poverty research and policy with evidence that demands deep and critical reflection.

We have come a long way with poverty studies and the analysis and measurement of poverty. Only 20 years ago the concept of income-poverty was almost a monoculture, reinforced in its dominance by being measurable and widely measured. In the 2010s it is still widespread, and useful for comparisons, but the multidimensionality of poverty is today accepted and not seriously questioned. We now have numerous concepts, indicators and composite indices to describe and measure it. Exclusion, deprivation, vulnerability and ill-being are all part of the broader vocabulary now used for aspects of the bad life. It is much more acceptable now to ask: whose concepts of poverty? 'Ours' – those of professionals, or 'theirs' – those of poor people? *Poverty and Development in China* confronts these questions and then takes us much further. Any sense that we have arrived, and now know enough about poverty and its identification, can in no way survive this book.

Its unique strength is that Caizhen Lu applied and compared four alternative approaches to poverty assessment to the same households in the same four villages in Yunnan Province. The first alternative was the official poverty list drawn up by village officials and leaders for submission upwards, in due course to be linked with benefits from the system. She describes the actual process, how it differed from the required government procedure, and the consequences. The second was the monetary poverty approach based on expenditure, and then separately on income, and assessed at various cut-off points. The third was participatory poverty assessment with focus groups and participatory wealth ranking. And the fourth was the use of multidimensional poverty indicators. Some of these concepts and measures were used for the first time in China.

The quality of the research and the critical reflections on methodology and epistemology make the findings highly credible. Description and review of the four methodologies are valuable contributions for the whole field of poverty studies. Even-handedly Lu Caizhen considers the pros and cons of each approach. To take one example, she recognizes the strengths of participatory poverty assessment and finds, contrary to some common belief, that it costs less than household surveys and saves time; but she also recognizes its limitations for generalization.

The comparison of what was learnt through the four approaches gives us a richness of description. There is here a treasury of detail about poverty and the realities of life in contemporary rural China. Much of this is also relevant for poverty elsewhere. The findings go beyond the better known dimensions, as when people's own indicators of poverty include the number of bachelors in a household, and many old women are found to be at their wits' end with a life that is not only lonely but boring.

The book leads to a devastating climax. I hesitate to mention it for fear of spoiling the discovery for others. But it is so significant and dramatic that I must flag it lest it be missed. After her painstaking and meticulous research, Lu Caizhen compares the households found to be poor by the four alternative approaches. The result is stunning. Less than 1 per cent, only 4 out of the 473, was identified by all four approaches. Not only that, but those in common between any two or three approaches were far fewer than might have been expected. That these findings present major challenges to research, policy and practice is starkly self-evident.

So this book raises huge questions about paradigmatic syndromes of methodology, epistemology and policy. Different approaches not only point to different people as poor but they embody different values, and they lead to different conclusions about what should be done. Most obviously, the monetary poverty approach leads to policies to generate income and for infrastructure, as the author points out, to the neglect of education, health and pensions. After this book, things can never be, or should never be, the same. For it shows with scholarship, elegance and rigour that we cannot evade the need, in the interest of poor and deprived people themselves, for critical epistemological awareness to recognize how our methods inform and maintain our mindsets and how this affects the policies and practices that are advocated and adopted.

Let me hope that *Poverty and Development in China* will be widely available at an accessible price. For it should be on every reading list for poverty studies in all countries, North and South, and should be considered by policy-makers in China and elsewhere. It is rare that we are presented with such a feast of insight and such a frontal challenge. We have to appreciate 'the politics of epistemology'. To understand poverty, and to know what best to do, we have to look back on ourselves and our methods of inquiry. After this book, unless its readership is restricted by price, there is no excuse for any lack of reflexivity about approaches, even less for methodological monoculture. Poverty studies should never be quite the same again.

Source: Caizhen Lu (2012) Poverty and Development in China: Alternative approaches to poverty assessment. London: Routledge.

Reflections from Tami Blumenfield

> *Tami Blumenfield, PhD, MLIS, is a sociocultural anthropologist, filmmaker, and gender expert with over two decades of experience in south-west China. She first encountered Robert Chambers' work while completing an International Development Policy and Management Certificate at the University of Washington. In 2005 she helped launch the Cool Mountain Education Fund, which bolstered Nuosu students and their educators in a small pocket of rural Sichuan until conditions improved substantially and political circumstances necessitated ending operations. From incorporation until the 2022 closure, Dr Blumenfield served on the board in many capacities, including three years as President. She is now a Kui Ge Scholar at Yunnan University.*

'After this book, things can never be ... the same': Introducing Caizhen Lu and Poverty and Development in China (2012)

When Caizhen Lu conducted research about defining and identifying poverty in south-west China, from 2005 to 2006, the People's Republic was in a very different position than it is today. Back then, a lengthy period of disinvestment by the central government in services like healthcare and education, with the expectation that regional and local governments would absorb the costs and fund them with some help from fees from users, was only gradually giving way to a return to state investment. The 1980s had ushered in an abrupt shift from the high socialist era (approximately 1949–1978), when these services had been heavily subsidized, and the human costs were intense.

Planned birth policies were still in effect, and families with limited resources were choosing to send their sickly baby boys to the doctor quickly but forgoing immediate medical care for their female counterparts. Instead, they waited to see whether the girls would improve on their own. And many young people from rural areas decided to jump straight from primary schooling into a labour market ravenous for warm bodies. East coast factories, urban hotels and restaurants, and construction sites throughout the country all needed them. While wages were not enormous if we consider them strictly from a monetary perspective, they were fortunes nonetheless to the young people whose housing and food were already covered. They could suddenly afford to buy stylish consumer items, contribute to siblings' school fees (Poras, 2014), and help pay medical bills that easily amounted to several years' annual income for rural families (Luo, 2008: 27–28).

Now the situation is very different. Beginning with the New Socialist Countryside project, and accelerating under the Xi Jinping regime, China has shifted from expecting all regions and localities to support their own needs, to recognizing that uneven resources and divergent levels of capital investment, along with difficult topography that makes travel challenging or impossible during parts of the year, make this expectation unrealistic. Developing infrastructure and connecting far-off regions have been major endeavours, in a domestic version of the oft-discussed Belt and Road Initiative. Perilous, multiday journeys with pack animals along mountain trails have largely been replaced by somewhat safer hours-long ones, with gasoline-fuelled vehicles on actual roads (Blumenfield et al., 2018). Medical insurance is now provided to nearly everyone with household registrations that match their locality. Although rural residents must pay a larger share of their bills than urban ones, fewer families face the agonizing situation of having no choice but to watch their loved ones die, for want of funds to pay for care. And nearly everyone completes primary school, where 'nutritious lunch' and textbooks are provided without charge in higher-poverty regions (at least in theory), and a much larger proportion of rural students continues to middle school than ever before (Wang et al. 2018, Yue et al. 2018). An ambitious campaign to eliminate poverty by the year 2020 compelled enormous investments in both person resources and financial resources. And its goal was declared accomplished: in a grand proclamation during February 2021, Xi Jinping announced that China had eradicated poverty completely.

And this becomes our cue to return to Caizhen Lu's important 2012 work, which tested definitions and frameworks for identifying poverty in the same few villages among the same sets of people and found they produced wildly different results. For, can it truly be possible in a nation as vast as China, home to legendary mountains and harsh desert climates, to flood-prone lowlands and an incredible diversity of peoples and places, that not a single person out of 1.4 billion remains impoverished?

No, of course not. An elderly man froze to death in a friend of a friend's village despite the end-of-poverty declaration. Other stories also underscore the continuing struggles people encounter. A huge number of people who would otherwise be considered impoverished began receiving regular cash transfers and other forms of assistance. When these eventually end, will it have been enough?

Already the 'poverty alleviation' offices tasked with meeting the 2020 goal have taken down their placards and reinstalled them with new names: they are now known as offices of 'rural revitalization'. To the seasoned and cynical anthropologist, this sounds suspiciously like old wine in new bottles. As much as we want to believe that the war against poverty has truly succeeded, as much as we hope that people's newly provided housing arrangements (distributed as part of the anti-poverty efforts) will meet their social as well as livelihood-related needs, we have heard too many stories of people unable to adjust from mountain living to the apartment-tower lifestyle, where landlessness makes farming impossible, to find this credible. Which brings us back to definitions. How to define poverty, and what elements besides cash, income, and property-based ones should be included in these definitions, remains a critically important question. We might ask Caizhen Lu to once again bring out those long-ago criteria and return to the original villages for some follow-up investigations. Using any of the four metrics used in the mid-2000s, has poverty truly vanished?[1] Will these frameworks once again produce wildly divergent lists of who 'qualifies' as impoverished, of who gets to receive the honour of being designated an official 'poor' family? And if impoverished individuals and families do still exist, how can they even be discussed in this new era when 'poverty' has become the name-that-shall-not-be-named, even if efforts to ameliorate it still need to occur? These are important questions to consider, even if the project may threaten to diminish the enthusiastic declarations of recent years. We eagerly await Dr Lu's follow-up project, and Professor Chambers' introduction to that future work.

Note

1. The four methods are 'official poverty line' (OPL), 'national poverty line' (NPL), 'participatory wealth ranking', and use of 'multidimensional poverty indicators' (MDI) (Lu, 2012: 1).

References

Blumenfield, T., Sum, C.-Y., Shenk, M.K., and Mattison, S.M. (2018). 'Poverty alleviation and mobility in southwest China: Examining effects of market transition and state policies in Mosuo communities'. *Urban Anthropology and Studies of Cultural Systems and World Economic Development* 47(3,4): 259–299. http://www.jstor.org/stable/45172910

Lu, C. (2012). *Poverty and Development in China: Alternative approaches to poverty assessment*. London: Routledge.

Luo, C.-L. (2008). *The Gender Impact of Modernization among the Matrilineal Moso in China*. MA thesis, Institute of Social Studies, The Hague, The Netherlands.

Poras, M. (2014). *The Mosuo Sisters*. ITVS. https://itvs.org/films/mosuo-sisters

Wang, L. Li, M., Abbey, M., and Rozelle, S. 2018. Human Capital and the Middle Income Trap: How Many of China's Youth are Going to High School? *The Developing Economies* 56(2): 82–103.

Yue, A., Tang, B., Shi, Y., Tang, J., Shang, G., Medina, A. and Rozelle, S. 2018. Rural education across China's 40 years of reform: past successes and future challenges. *China Agricultural Economic Review* 10(1): 93–118. https://doi.org/10.1108/CAER-11-2017-0222

Foreword to *Wellbeing and Quality of Life Assessment: A practical guide* (2014) by Sarah C. White with Asha Abeyasekera

As well as Robert's foreword here, we have two reflection pieces, one from Rosalind Willi, which engages directly with the text, and contextualizes the measurement of wellbeing within both contemporary developments and her own doctoral research. And another, from Jackie Shaw, who asks what a juxtaposition between wellbeing and Healing Justice might do, to re-politicize wellbeing as a concept.

Over the past two decades wellbeing and quality of life have become part of the rhetoric of development. This has been a positive trend, for these words and concepts make space for and accommodate the multi-dimensionality of the good life to which we aspire for ourselves and for others. This book brings together a range of pioneering initiatives to explore these concepts in practice. Comparing and analysing these shows that wellbeing and quality of life raise puzzles and challenges and present opportunities.

One challenge is the tension between universal 'objective' measures, like those in Human Development Reports, and the reality that what people seek and value as wellbeing is subjective and varies by person, gender, age, relationships, status, place, culture and more. And subjective experiences of wellbeing are also not static but continuously evolve.

Another is that every language has its equivalent collection of words and expressions for wellbeing, all of which have different connotations and are dynamic and change over time. In English, as in this book, there is a plurality of expressions which to varying degrees are synonymous: wellbeing (used on its own, or defined or qualified as inner, responsible, physical, psychosocial or personal wellbeing), quality of life, happiness, good and happy life, human flourishing ... Given this pluralism, a big question is then who defines wellbeing? And for whom? Do professionals define for other people, or are people convened and facilitated to define for themselves? Pervasively, these are the questions to be asked in framing wellbeing: whose language, whose meanings, whose categories, whose concepts, whose values, whose indicators (in these and other dimensions), and whose realities count? 'Ours', those of us who intervene, convene and facilitate? Or 'theirs', those of local participants?

This practical guide helps the reader to navigate these difficult waters and to recognise that the questions are important and the answers not easy. The nuanced reflections to be found here throw light on some of the difficulties and dilemmas. The challenge is to identify, test and evolve processes and procedures to empower people to analyse and express for themselves their ideas of the good life, or good conditions of life, or the words and expressions they use for these. There is no one answer. But whatever their methodology, contributors stress one thing: that sensitive facilitation is vital to enable participants to reflect on their own multi-faceted meanings and to share these without distortion.

Hitherto, the initiatives to elicit personal, local and cultural ideas of wellbeing have been scattered and largely isolated. This book takes us forward into a new space, not only by framing the debate with the current state of understanding, as it does in the first three chapters, but by bringing together different approaches and methods. As readers, we are then presented not with a fixed menu but with an *à la carte* selection of approaches and combinations of methods. Each methodology can be a source of ideas for inventive adaptation, as in cooking a dish for a specific need and context. Any reader wishing to use a wellbeing and quality of life approach can adopt one of the methodologies presented here, or can treat them as sources of ingredients, of ideas, of methods that can be adopted, mixed and adapted, or used as raw material or inspiration for innovation, or as the basis for improvisation or invention. This book can then be taken as an invitation for creativity.

The opportunities opened up are significant. The utility and potentials of a focus on wellbeing and using approaches like those presented here are many-sided. They provide means for escaping the reductionism of any one discipline, whether economics or any other. They enable many people to gain from reflecting on their values and ideals of the good life. Being facilitated for such reflection can itself be a positive intervention which leaves participants with insights, changed relationships and on-going processes: wellbeing analysis then itself enhances the wellbeing of those who participate. Outsiders who facilitate gain understandings that would otherwise be largely inaccessible, and which may better orient their activities. And the values local people express in describing their ideas of wellbeing can be credible and persuasive indicators for assessing the impact of interventions. They can combine in one measure or comparison how people feel subjectively, which has validity in terms of what really matters to them, adding to, qualifying and complementing conventional 'objective' indicators. And strikingly from these accounts, these approaches are win-win: participants find them of value, generating reflecting and change; and facilitators find them of significant interest and sources of insight.

Let me congratulate the editors and contributors for their pioneering courage and diverse and inventive approaches. They deserve thanks for what the rest of us can learn from them: from their accounts of their experiences and their critical reflections on strengths and limitations. And let me hope that through the inspiration of this book many more development initiatives will focus on wellbeing as a key dimension of good change, so that we can learn from local people what they want for themselves and their children and give that priority.

Source: White, S.C. with Abeyasekera, A. (2014). *Wellbeing and Quality of Life Assessment: A practical guide*. Rugby: Practical Action Publishing.

Reflections from Rosalind Willi

> *Rosalind is a doctoral researcher at IDS. Her doctoral research employs ethnographic and participatory child-centred methods to look at child wellbeing understandings and strategies among Syrian-Armenian communities in Armenia, in the context of development interventions. Rosalind has more than 10 years of experience as a research and development practitioner in child protection, in local and international NGOs in contexts such as Austria, Armenia, Bulgaria, Georgia, Lebanon, and South Africa. While unfortunately she has never had the chance to meet Robert, she is closely engaging with Sarah White's wellbeing concept in the frame of her PhD.*

'Who defines wellbeing? And for whom?': Exploring child wellbeing understandings

The reflections by White, Abeyasekera, and Chambers on the challenges as well as opportunities of the focus on wellbeing in development interventions are as pertinent today as when the book *Wellbeing and Quality of Life Assessment: A practical guide* was published in 2014. While in recent years predominant wellbeing measures have become more multidimensional, there is still a strong focus on wellbeing as an outcome of the individual which is externally defined, rather than as a process which happens in relationship and is locally constituted and determined (White 2010, 2016, 2018).

Exploring how wellbeing meanings come about and how people navigate them can help mediate some of these challenges (White 2016). This can unmask the relational hierarchies of power Chambers so pertinently highlights when asking: '…who defines wellbeing? And for whom?' His concluding sentence: 'And let me hope that through the inspiration of this book many more development initiatives will focus on wellbeing as a key dimension of good change, so that we can learn from local people what they want for themselves and their children and give that priority' made me reflect on my own research that focuses on children's wellbeing in the context of mobility and development interventions.

In my research I came to understand that what families want for their children, what development actors want for (migrant) children, and most importantly, what children want for themselves and their families to live 'a good life' (White 2018) are sometimes quite contradictory. Wellbeing understandings are not only highly relational across different local and international actors, but even across children and adults within a given family (Crivello et al. 2009). How child wellbeing is understood is informed by individual as well as collective understandings related to childhood, which shift across time, place, and space and are mediated by age, gender, and generation. Moreover, child wellbeing understandings are strongly influenced by 'the perspectives and practices of institutions' that shape children and their families' lives (Tiilikainen et al. 2020: 2). Exploring 'how accounts of wellbeing are produced' (White 2016: 3) provides insights into different emic understandings related to what it means to be a 'good' child, parent, family, and migrant, which come together in development interventions that aim to improve child wellbeing.

As pointed out by Chambers, the 'opportunities opened up are significant', in that wellbeing as a concept allows for the exploration of and dialogue about these various 'values and ideals' and tensions therein. It can help development practitioners and researchers alike to 'listen long and well enough' (White 2018: 16) to understand the wellbeing expectations that children are navigating in their daily lives. Putting children's wellbeing visions and their dreams for future 'wellbecoming' (Phoenix 2020) at the centre could not only considerably improve the effectiveness of development interventions to enhance their wellbeing. It could also enable the needed shift from objectifying and individualizing children's lives, towards seeing them as subjects in a complex web of social relationships that they are navigating as they strive towards what wellbeing means for them (White 2018).

Reflections from Jackie Shaw

Jackie Shaw is a social psychologist (PhD. LSE) and multidisciplinary researcher with key expertise using participatory, creative methodologies to mediate inclusive research and collective change processes. Following 30+ years' experience in diverse community, development, and health contexts, she is Senior Research Fellow at the

Institute of Development Studies. *She convenes multi-county research collaborations with marginalized people in highly inequitable, insecure, and unaccountable contexts – currently exploring social assistance with disabled people and other excluded groups in Iraq and Uganda. She recently led innovative research on Healing Justice and collective healing as radical organizing strategies for feminist activists in Africa.*

Re-politicizing wellbeing: Towards Healing Justice as a radical approach to feminist activism

Wellbeing and the allied concept of quality of life are multidimensional, incorporating material, subjective, bio-psycho-social, relational, and dynamic aspects. They have always had political dimensions within international development as positive psychological aspirations and because they connect self-efficacy and collective agency and action. The value of concepts lies in their real-world function in driving discourse and action, and White and Abeyasekera's (2014) *Wellbeing and Quality of Life Assessment: A practical guide* focuses on the utility of wellbeing in focusing us on the impact of development interventions from people's subjective perspectives, as well as their experiences of the issues they face and the broader effects on their families, peers, and wider communities. This is reflected in Robert's foreword, in which he asks whose understanding of wellbeing matters. He emphasizes the fundamental importance of involving diverse people in particular contexts in exploring what a good life means for them, and in evolving and assessing processes to bring about their desired changes towards greater happiness and life satisfaction.

Both wellbeing and quality of life have 'objective' and 'subjective' aspects, and Robert also highlights the tensions generated by universal 'fixed' measures, and the fluid, processual nature of these concepts. White and Abeyasekera's book responds to these tensions epistemologically and methodologically, by shifting the focus of wellbeing evaluations from material circumstances and achievements (in economics, education, housing, health, inclusion, or governance, for example), towards the impact on peoples' lived realities as an ongoing matter. This centres local priorities, subjective affects, relationships between people, and the need to navigate power dynamics over time.

Given the evidenced knowledge that it is often contextual, emotional, relational, dynamic, and other tacit subjective factors that contribute to the failure of development interventions (e.g. Shaw et al. 2020); the consequent prioritization of lived experiences within development research; and the explicit highlighting of critical empowerment as a key wellbeing dimension; it is somewhat surprising that this concept has not been more prominent in mainstream development discourse in the decade since this foreword was published. However, it is highly pertinent to the call to *Build Back Better* after the Covid-19 health pandemic, and the subsequent questions about what sustainable, inclusive, or 'good' growth/progress means, incorporating values such as social justice, diversity, and pluralism, environmental protection, and the fulfilment of human potential.

Robert states that wellbeing should be a key to 'good' change, and this resonates currently with the intentions of Healing Justice – an emerging radical approach to activism that has been applied by Black Lives Matter and other contemporary social movements.

Healing justice seeks to address the systemic injustice and harm experienced by marginalized peoples. It recognizes that oppressive histories and structural violence generate intergenerational and collective traumas, which manifest in negative physical, mental–emotional, and spiritual effects for activists and their movements. Importantly, healing justice points forwards to improving the wellbeing of activists and their movements, through transforming the cultures and relations of activism and explicitly prioritizing collective healing practices as core movement work. However, healing justice should be contextualized by those living the issues, as Robert surely would agree, and this provided the rationale for a recent research project exploring what Healing Justice means to feminist activists in different African contexts, from a political rather than medical standpoint (see Shaw et al. 2022). I was excited to be part of this research as it brought together my past experiences in social psychology, complementary healing modalities, participatory research, and feminist activism, but, responding to Robert's posed question, this project was not about externally imposed ideas or practices, but activists and healers in different African contexts themselves deciding how wellbeing could be fostered for individuals and in the social bodies of their movements.

This study contributes to re-politicizing wellbeing firstly by locating Healing Justice as a transformative feminist approach that seeks to address the 'ghosts of historical injustice' (Amadiume and An-Na'im 2000) by evolving better circumstances, not merely holding feminist activists safe or helping them cope (Shaw et al. 2022: 29–34, 55–65). *Collective trauma* refers to the impacts from historical events or ongoing circumstances, which manifest similarly in the present for many people across a context. As with material responses to promoting wellbeing, our research participants illustrated the ineffectiveness of individualized and medicalized healing approaches, which do not address the pathological systems at the root of oppression, discrimination, and poverty, or the resultant 'social' sicknesses. Healing justice therefore politicizes pathways to wellbeing as it assumes collective trauma requires collective healing responses. And, as structural violence is perpetuated in activists' lives through micro-level power relations, collective healing is anticipated to be tackled with intersectional awareness from *within* movements. The personal is political as the feminist adage goes.

As with other development concerns such as multidimensional poverty and empowerment, people's subjective experiences of wellbeing encompass more than material and measurable circumstances. Responding to the embodied manifestations of collective trauma, collective healing, like wellbeing (White 2010), goes beyond recognition of multidimensionality to explicitly work across different aspects by incorporating both holistic healing and political organizing practices that connect body–mind–emotion–spirit. Grounded in our research context by African health epistemologies, this also acknowledges the disharmonious relationships between environment, community, family, ancestors, and natural spirits that can cause distress (Bojuwoye and Moletsane-Kekae 2018), and suggests how healing processes might unfold towards social and political healing (Shaw et al. 2022: 67–87).

Robert's foreword highlights that prioritizing wellbeing is not about measuring fixed realities, but ongoing social processes towards better lives (White 2010). He draws our attention to the opportunity to draw on and adapt the range of methodologies in the guidebook. In a comparable way, healing justice assumes the healing journeys of each feminist activist and movement is unique, but also identifies some common foundational elements and practices that could be combined or weaved together adaptively as appropriate to foster 'healthier' and thus stronger and more sustainable feminist organizing.

In summary, healing justice and collective healing illustrate politicized routes to improving wellbeing that have emerged bottom-up and play out in relationships between the individual and the collective. They function as social psychological drivers with a positive orientation towards potencies rather than shortfalls; for example, they are not about assessing deficits, but kindling hope and positive energy to generate future possibilities. This resonates with White and Abeyasekera's practical orientation to the purpose of wellbeing in encouraging ground-led change, which I trust would give Robert satisfaction.

References

Amadiume, I. and An-Na'im, M. (2000). *The Politics of Memory: Truth, healing, and social justice*, New York: Zed Books.

Bojuwoye, O. and Moletsane-Kekae, M. (2018). 'African indigenous knowledge systems and healing traditions'. In S. Fernando and R. Moodley (eds), *Global Psychologies*, London: Palgrave Macmillan. pp. 77–98.

Crivello, G., Camfield, L., and Woodhead, M. (2009). 'How can children tell us about their wellbeing? Exploring the potential of participatory research approaches within young lives'. *Social Indicators Research* 90(1): 51–72. https://doi.org/10.1007/s11205-008-9312-x

Phoenix, A. (2020). 'Childhood, wellbeing, and transnational migrant families: Conceptual and methodological issues'. In M. Tiilikainen, M. Al-Sharmani, and S. Mustasaari (eds), *Wellbeing of Transnational Muslim Families. Marriage, Law and Gender*, pp. 164–82, London: Routledge. https://doi.org/10.4324/9781315231976-10

Shaw, J., Howard, J., and Lopez Franco, E. (2020) 'Building inclusive community activism and accountable relations through an intersecting inequalities approach', *Community Development Journal* No 55: 1 pp. 7–25.

Shaw, J., Amir, M., and Lewin, T., with Kemitare, J., Diop, A., Kithumbu, O., Mupotsa, D., and Odiase, S. (2022). *Contextualising Healing Justice as a Feminist Organising Framework in Africa*, IDS Working Paper 576, Brighton: Institute of Development Studies. https://doi.org/10.19088/IDS.2022.063

Tiilikainen, M., Al-Sharmani, M., and Mustasaari, S. (eds.) (2020). *Wellbeing of Transnational Muslim Families: Marriage, law and gender*. London: Routledge.

White, S.C. (2010). 'Analysing wellbeing: A framework for development practice'. *Development in Practice* 20(2): 158–72. https://doi.org/10.1080/09614520903564199

White, S. (2016). 'Introduction: The many faces of wellbeing'. In C. Blackmore and S. White (eds.), *Cultures of Wellbeing: Method, Place, Policy*. Palgrave Macmillan UK.

White, S.C. (2018). *Moralities of Wellbeing. Bath Papers in International Development and Wellbeing*. No. 58. Centre for Development Studies, University of Bath.

White, S.C. with Abeyasekera, A. (2014). *Wellbeing and Quality of Life Assessment: A practical guide*. Rugby: Practical Action Publishing.

Foreword to *Participation Pays: Pathways for post-2015* (2015) edited by Tom Thomas and Pradeep Narayanan

> *From what I understand, Robert was instrumental in 'nudging' Tom and Pradeep towards writing this book, and certainly in assuring them of its importance. Praxis had been doing participatory development work for decades, most of it undocumented. This book is an attempt to capture some of this work.*

It is an honour to have been invited to write a foreword for this remarkable, important, timely and inspiring book.

It is remarkable because it presents key experiences and learning of remarkable people in a remarkable organization. Praxis is an NGO which has been at the forefront of participatory practice for over two decades. It is deeply committed to ideals of equity and justice: as this book illustrates so eloquently through reflective accounts of eight of its major activities, it has aligned itself with those who are poor, marginalized and discriminated against, working with them, and enabling them to gain for themselves respect, their rights and a better life. Praxis has engaged mainly in India and with some of India's most intractable problems; and with the exception of the Maldives, all the chapters draw on Indian experience. What the book does not mention is that Praxis funds itself through commissioned projects like those recounted here, and uses its income not to reward staff but to build up a corpus to fund other activities, such as its participatory training work in Afghanistan. Also what cannot be shown here is the behaviour, attitudes, commitment, resolution and courage without which the experiences in these eight chapters would never have been achieved.

Participation Pays is important because it opens up and demonstrates frontiers for development practice. The authors describe much of what they do as subversive (latin *sub*, below and *vertere*, to turn). Consistently the actors in these pages are from *below*, the powerless, those on the social, economic, spatial and political margins. So here we can learn from subaltern, subordinated groups – the landless in Bihar, those robbed of homes, livelihoods and land by the tsunami in the Maldives and Tamil Nadu, transgendered people, LGBTs, sex workers, injecting drug users, men having sex with men, and pervasively again and again in different contexts women and those facing caste discrimination. We read how Praxis *turns* normal top–down power relations on their heads. Those 'below' are sought out, respected, listened to, facilitated to do their own appraisal and analysis, and their priorities and realities are then put first. And when this is done, again and again, they show capabilities – in participatory mapping of land, in conducting their own censuses, in wellbeing ranking, in analysing power relations, designing and building their own new homes, in carrying out evaluations, in facilitating their peers to do likewise – far beyond what many development professionals suppose.

Participation Pays is timely because it is being published in the watershed year of 2015 when the MDGs come to an end and the SDGs (sustainable development goals) start. The MDGs 'picked the low-hanging fruit', that is, the targets that could most cheaply and conveniently be achieved through gains by those whom it was easiest to reach, not through those who were less easy, weaker, more marginal and worse off. SDG rhetoric stresses equity and equality, holding promise that the focus will shift to those who are poorest, most stigmatized, excluded and marginalized, least able to help themselves, and most isolated; in short, those who are 'last'. These are precisely those with whom Praxis has been engaged for two decades, opening up and exploring pathways to 2015, making this book so timely and the subtitle *Pathways for post-2015* so apposite.

How participation pays fits the new goals. For empowering those who are powerless, participation is both indispensable and cost-effective. There is no substitute. But it is not a solution to be taken off the shelf. It has to be lived. It has to be part of a mindset and a way of life. So let those who read this book not be misled. It is all too easy and common for those who talk of participation to neglect power and the personal dimension. NGOs widely adopt participatory rhetoric and write nice proposals, but many are gatekeepers and claim to speak for those who are poor and marginalized rather than enabling and empowering them to act and speak for themselves. Power relations have to be reversed through personal and institutional commitment and action and resisting the top–down reporting and accountability demands of donors. If downward accountability is not part of the SDGs, then in the interests of those the SDGs are meant to serve it must be fought for. Participatory non-negotiables, like those of Praxis, need to be debated, agreed and asserted, to become stronger and more accepted in balancing development relationships.

Participation Pays is inspiring because it gives us hope that we can make our world a better place. The barrage of bad news that assaults us daily neglects the good news. And here the good news is evidence that much can be achieved against the odds if only we have the guts and vision to try. Those who illegally controlled land in Bihar could be confronted. Those who sought to exploit the post-tsunami opportunity to seize land and water for hotels and shrimp farming could be opposed. Poor, marginalized and stigmatized people could do much more than most professionals would have supposed. Again and again, asking who? and whose? questions – whose knowledge, whose appraisal, whose analysis, whose priorities, whose indicators, whose monitoring and evaluation, whose realities, whose theory of change? – these and many other questions can be answered by 'theirs' rather than 'ours'. And 'we' often have power to empower, not least by convening occasions, and bringing poor people and those with power together, showing how their values and priorities differ, as with the Ground-level Panel which Praxis convened to influence the post-2015 agenda.

Praxis deserves praise for what it has shown can be done, for its self-critical modesty, and for sharing what it has learnt. May the pathways it has opened up, explored and shared encourage and embolden others, not to follow in their footsteps, but to blaze their own trails and to do this with the similar courage and commitment. Another world is possible. As President Obama so memorably said before his first election, 'Yes we can'. What Praxis has shown is that what we can do is more than many have believed.

Source: Thomas, T. and Narayanan, P. (2015) Participation Pays: Pathways for post-2015. Rugby: Practical Action Publishing

Reflections from Tom Thomas

> *Tom Thomas is a development worker, researcher, trainer, and observer. Since 2000, he has been the CEO of the organization Praxis – Institute for Participatory Practices in Chennai, India. Prior to this he worked in various capacities at ActionAid, including as the country director for ActionAid Bangladesh from 1989 to 1999. Tom is a long-time friend and collaborator of Robert's.*

The book *Participation Pays: Pathways for post-2015*, is both the evidence and the expectation from and of the several thousands of people whose lived experience, voices, and hope it echoes, underscoring the power of community engagement and active participation in shaping a sustainable future. For years, we have felt that this book needed to be written, but like many field practitioners, we too stayed in our comfort zone of being fully immersed in our community work rather than taking the time to reflect and document our experiences. The hype around the making of the SDGs and, even more importantly, Robert Chambers' persistent nudging ultimately made this book a reality. Writing this book was an enriching experience for all of us, team Praxis and Praxis as an institution. We also believe that it is a partial settlement of an inherent debt to the communities – the commitment to amplifying their voices. The insights and perspectives shared in this book remain just as relevant today as they were when first written. In an era marked by growing inequality and threats to democratic ideals, the importance of active participation in shaping a better world cannot be overstated. As Robert says in his foreword, it is 'indispensable' and 'there is no substitute'. And 'it is not a solution to be taken off the shelf', 'it has to be lived'.

Preface to *Can We Know Better? Reflections for development* (2017) by Robert Chambers

Can We Know Better *builds on several of Robert's previous publications in critiquing the orthodoxies held by international development donors and practitioners, which he argues tend to privilege a Newtonian paradigm (better for things) that oversimplifies social realities, over a complexity paradigm (better for people). The first half critiques the field and explores numerous development failures. The second half suggests multiple ways of 'knowing better'.*

'Certainty is the greatest of all illusions ... it is what the ancients meant by *hubris*. The only certainty, it seems to me, is that those who believe they are certainly right are certainly wrong.'

Iain McGilchrist, *The Master and his Emissary* (2009: 460)

'Now, *here*, you see, it takes all the running you can do, to keep in the same place. If you want to get somewhere else, you must run at least twice as fast as that!'

Lewis Carroll, *Alice Through the Looking Glass*

'Start, stumble, self-correct, share.'

Precept from participatory rural appraisal in the 1990s

Context and direction

This is a challenging and thrilling time to be alive, active, and engaged with development. So much has changed and is changing so fast. Potentials for making a difference grow. Rapid change and communication mean that small strategic actions can have big impacts later. Negatively, the worse things are, and since drafting this preface in 2016 they have become much worse, the greater can be the scope for making them less bad. Positively, it is a galvanizing opportunity to be confronted by so much to keep up with, so much to learn and unlearn, and so many new domains of knowledge continuously opening up. At the same time, many of us are so bombarded and overstimulated by digital information and demands that little time is left to stand back and reflect critically on how we know and how we might know better. This has made it a privilege to have had the time and support to write this book.

It is thrilling too because meanings of 'development' continuously evolve and diversify. I use it to mean 'good change', applying this to humankind universally. Past is the time when it referred just to developing countries. The 17 Sustainable Development Goals (SDGs) apply everywhere. All countries have signed up to them. The old dichotomies and mindsets of donor–recipient, North–South, developed–developing are superseded. In the spirit of the SDGs, *Can We Know Better?* is for all in all countries who work on or wish to contribute to the goals and what they stand for, and to achieve justice, equality, sustainability, security, and a better life for all now and in the future. For the present, we have the wonderful opportunities of living and working in new ways in new spaces of reciprocity, and mutual learning and sharing.

In this context, I question and challenge much in prevailing professionalism. I have been struck by the scale and depth of what I have found: that error, myth, biases, and blind spots are deeply endemic; that widely accepted and required procedures, approaches, and concepts of rigour distort vision and diminish effectiveness; that the power of funding often carries conditions that misfit complex realities and incur high hidden costs. There are successes to celebrate, not least the explosion of participatory methodologies. But many well-intended actions in the name of development miss the mark. I present evidence that development practice has been driven further and further in a damaging direction. The issues here are at once epistemological, paradigmatic, and practical.

Those whose lives much of the rhetoric of development aims to improve – those who are poor, vulnerable, marginalized, weak, displaced, insecure, stigmatized, excluded, powerless, those left out and left behind – in sum, all those who are 'last' – deserve that those of us who are not last learn to know better and be more in touch and up to date with their realities, and more committed and fired with passion to know the truth and to do better. Those who are last, and those of us who are not last, are to be found in all countries. To make our rhetoric real cries out for a revolution in development knowing, thinking, and practice everywhere. We have to transform how we see things, how we behave, how we interact, how we learn and know, and what we do.

Self-critical reflexivity

Self-critical reflexivity is at the core of knowing better. So, I must start with myself and explain the drivers behind this book. Let me warn you about biases, predispositions, and errors that I recognize in myself and in the origins and content of this book. I mention others in the text and yet more you will notice in your reading.

As I perceive it, writing this book has been driven (and no doubt distorted) by a mix of anger, frustration, curiosity, and enthusiasm. The anger verging on disbelief is at the grotesque and growing inequalities of our world, the ideology of greed and the stupidity and short-sightedness that so widely prevail, the dishonesty, fake news and lies glossed as 'alternative facts' that are now widespread, reminiscent of Ribbentrop and Orwell's Ministry of Truth, and the mean xenophobia that has spread in a world with an unimaginable scale of suffering from wars, famine, and injustice. I am angry too with myself for the hypocrisy of my life and feeble responses. The frustration is with the dead hand of professional conservatism and its academic and bureaucratic reproduction through values, incentives, procedures, habits, and mindsets that condition, constrain, distort, and blinker perceptions and practice, so often leading to blindness, errors, and bad ways of doing things.

My curiosity and enthusiasm stem from a fascination with evidence, which allows me the fond delusion that I have a passion for truth, tracing this to a background in natural sciences and history. In university I studied the unification of Italy where evidence conflicted, some had been forged, myths had been generated, and actors' motivations were complex and inscrutable. It was fascinating trying to get closer to elusive realities. At times the only reasonable conclusion was that we did not know and could never know. Which now may apply to more of this book than I care to recognize. But again and again it has been exciting to explore how we 'know' and how we get things wrong. It has been enthralling to search, drawing on others' experience, for better ways of knowing and doing and getting closer to truth, and to know eureka moments of ah-ha!

In none of this am I 'holier than thou'. Looking back at almost six decades of personal engagement with 'development', I recognize that I have often and for long periods been seriously wrong while sure that I was right (see Chambers, 2014). Experience as a decolonizing administrator and trainer in Kenya left me with top-down attitudes and behaviours and a mindset which took long to recognize and unlearn. My authoritarian and unreflective management contributed to the failure of an evaluation I was in charge of in Kenya. The first books I wrote saw things and prescribed actions from the perspectives of managers, not those of the managed. Participation was little on my map. There is much in those earlier books that I now see as biased; and if I was wrong then, I am surely still wrong now, if in other ways.

In the first three chapters you may detect unjustified dogmatism: in gleefully detecting errors and myths in Chapter 1, identifying biases and blind spots in Chapter 2, and exposing deficiencies of mechanistic processes and procedures in Chapter 3. You may sense that I am vulnerable to enjoying the sport of bank- and donor-baiting. I pose as balanced but have caught myself cherry picking evidence to support the case I wish to make. I have made corrections, for instance in qualifying my critique of mechanistic practices and procedures in Chapter 3, but errors of fact and judgement will surely remain. That said, I live in hope that readers will take on board the major points and perspectives.

The more positive and forward-looking second half of the book is infused with an optimism which negative academics may find naïve and those embedded in bureaucracies difficult to put into practice. As this goes to press events have unfolded which introduce new nastiness, irresponsibility, and danger into our world. This book should support all who stand for the human values of inclusiveness, honesty, respect, and love. I make no apologies for my hope and optimism. I am hard-wired to look for win–win solutions. This can lead me to underplay conflict situations which are zero sum. But I cannot help being thrilled by what I see as vast potentials for practical realism: for knowing and doing better in development through rigour for complexity (Chapter 4), participatory approaches and methods (Chapter 5), and reflexivity and facilitation (Chapter 6).

Despite my dogmatic style of writing, I remain full of doubts. The question mark in the title signals that the assertions throughout the book are provisional. Many sentences should end with question marks. My analysis of errors, myths, biases, and blind spots surely suffers from errors, myths, biases, and blind spots itself. These pages are the stumbling steps of one traveller on our collective journey in search of practical realism and what I dare to call truth. But realities and the truths about them continuously evolve. There is no final arrival. The future becomes ever less predictable. None of the conclusions here can be set in stone. All must be open to challenge. In our troubled and turbulent world, there will for ever be new constellations of being wrong and new ways of being right, of being in touch, up to date, and realistic. We will always need to go on learning how to know better, and through knowing better, doing better.

About this book

Writing this book has not been easy. It tries to cover a range of knowledges and practices, to critique mainstream conventions, and to propose practical alternatives. In the 15 years since I began it, our universe of knowing has transformed with astonishing speed. The explosion of digital and other technologies and their applications (Ramalingam et al., 2016) has been hard to keep up with, and the future of knowing has itself become less and less knowable. In the proverbial painting of the Forth Bridge, by the time one end was reached, the other needed repainting. In this case, the bridge has not only got longer and longer but has also all needed repainting all the time. Or as in Alice's world, to keep in touch and up to date I have needed to run ever faster and faster, updating and rewriting version after version of each of the chapters.

There is much this book is not. It is not primarily about how change happens: that is well covered in Duncan Green's book of that title, *How Change Happens* (2016). Nor is it primarily about foreign aid: a magisterial overview of the state of play with that is David Hulme's *Should Rich Nations Help the Poor?* (2016). Both these books are readable, engaging and accessible. Nor is it a handbook or manual of approaches and methods, though some of these are noted in Chapter 5. Neither is it a balanced review for development studies: for that, see Andy Sumner and Michael Tribe, *International Development Studies: Theories and methods in research and practice* (2008). Nor does it deal directly with some of the great issues of our time such as climate change, sustainability, insecurity, population growth, migration, refugees and displaced people, disarmament, xenophobia, archaic electoral systems, democratic and international governance, tax evasion, avoidance and havens, obscene and growing inequalities of wealth and income, or the many dimensions of injustice and abuses of human rights; and that is no more than a partial list.

What it does seek to do is raise questions about what we believe we know, what we do not know, and how we might come to know more and better and so see better what to do. The original title was *Knowing in Development* but this was too passive. A eureka breakthrough was when Clare Tawney of Practical Action Publishing suggested *Knowing Better*. This was more purposive and impelled me to rethink and rewrite with a more active orientation. This included adding agenda for action and reflection to each of the first five chapters. But the title still carried overtones of certainty and authority. Others helped with suggestions finally leading to *Can We Know Better?* The question invites you to reflect critically and to suggest yourself what can be done to take us closer to realities and truth.

Who this is for

I have written this ambitiously hoping it will be of interest and help to those who want to confront and correct the injustices and inequalities of our world and make it a better place for all. It is for development professionals, policymakers, politicians, officials, scientists, students, academics, religious leaders, freelancers, service providers, those who work in many departments and at many levels in many organisations, and all who are concerned and engaged with change for the better in all countries. We are people in government organizations, international agencies, NGOs, social movements, universities, colleges and schools, research and training institutes, faith organizations of all religions, the private sector, the media, and members of the general public from all walks of life and of all political persuasions. In the world we now live in, we are all in this together, interconnected as a new class. We cannot hide. We cannot escape responsibility. And with embarrassment I also address this to myself, and my own hubris and hypocrisy.

Let me now invite you into the book. The abstracts at the head of each chapter give a quick overview. The index and the chapter titles in the table of contents are to help you be selective. My hope is to shock, provoke, convince, and incite you to see and do things differently. The organization into six standalone chapters may lend itself to university, college and other courses, with six sessions, say one a week. Being open access, anyone can read or download these without cost.

A 'revolutionary new professionalism' may be hyperbole. Dream on, you may say. Well, I do dream. So, if words like normal, conventional, pedestrian, business as usual or nothing new come to mind as you read, I shall have failed. I want this book, however modestly, to help us to know better how to make our world a fairer, more equal, more secure, and fulfilling place, for all of us but mostly for those who are last. As long as our human race survives, there should be no end to knowing and doing and thrilling adventures of reflexive ground-truthing and exploration. Please read, criticize, improve on what is here, and enjoy.

Source: Chambers, R. (2017). Can We Know Better?: Reflections for Development. Rugby: Practical Action Publishing

References

Chambers, R. (2014) 'Critical reflections of a development nomad,' in my book *Into the Unknown*, Rugby, UK: Practical Action Publishing, 3–21.
Green, D. (2016) *How Change Happens*, Oxford University Press.
Hulme, D. (2016) *Should Rich Nations Help the Poor?*, Wiley.
McGilchrist, I. (2009) *The Master and his Emissary: The Divided Brain and the Making of the Western World*, New Haven, CT and London: Yale University Press.
Ramalingam, B., Hernandez, K., Prieto Martin, P. and Faith, B. (2016) *Ten Frontier Technologies for International Development*, Brighton, UK: Institute of Development Studies.

Sumner, A. and Tribe, M. (2008) *International Development Studies: Theories and Methods in Research and Practice*, Sage Books.

Chambers, R. (2017). *Can We Know Better?: Reflections for Development.* Rugby: Practical Action Publishing

Reflections from Jamie Myers

> *Jamie joined the Institute of Development Studies in 2014, working closely with Robert for several years, including while he was writing* Can We Know Better? *He is currently the Research and Learning Manager for the Sanitation Learning Hub and a PhD candidate at the University of Leeds undertaking research into peer learning and capacity strengthening in the sanitation sector. His work focuses on a range of different learning and research activities that support sanitation and hygiene programming, specializing in using participatory methods and learning processes which engage with different policy-makers, practitioners, and communities.*

Colleagues and I working for the Sanitation Learning Hub were lucky enough to work with Robert closely while *Can We Know Better?* was being written and he was instrumental in the design of the Hub and its former incarnations. It is consequently hard to distinguish between the book's Preface and the enormous contribution Robert has made to the project and myself as a mentor, colleague, and friend.

As Robert points out later in the book, the sanitation situation in many parts of the world is dire – currently 673 million people are reliant on open defecation – as well as complex, messy, and continually changing (improving and deteriorating). The need to understand people's lived realities, through adapting and evolving different methods to a given context is my first major take-away from the Preface, and central to our work.

What does this mean in the real world? It means working with people living in communities, identifying the barriers they face and asking them their priorities and solutions. In tandem, engaging with practitioners and policy-makers to identify questions and research and learning processes which can best support their work and help them to reflect on research findings, challenging them to consider how they can improve their practice. These activities should not be undertaken separately, each feeds into and informs the other.

Along with Robert, we evolved and use the term *Rapid Action Learning* which we define as tools (new and old) for policy-makers, practitioners, and researchers to use to be better in touch, engaged, and up to date with field realities; tools that support the creation of spaces for reflection and learning based on what is found. We find the terms *timely, relevant,* and *actionable* as useful criteria when designing research and learning processes. Providing findings in a *timely* manner to support decision-making; *relevant* in that it is up to date, context-specific, and adapted for the people we are working with; and *actionable* with specific recommendations proposed. Through this we are hopefully challenging ourselves to know better for and with knowledge users.

The second major take-away is the need to link this learning and research and learning about learning and research to self-critical reflexivity. There is a need to build in learning loops throughout the evolution of learning and research methodologies. We also need to revisit the aims and objectives or criteria for success, assessing if these have been met and considering if the aims and objectives and criteria are still of value and if we are still making a difference. This means as a team internally and at an individual level building in spaces and processes for learning and reflection. This has included learning diaries, reflective learning meetings, developing outcome monitoring processes to improve our programming, and acknowledging and addressing failures.

Robert starts every chapter with a quote, for this foreword of a preface, I would like to end with one of his from the book's final chapter:

> 'There will be so much to explore, so much to discover, so much to know, and so much to do.'(Chambers, 2017: 170).

Foreword to *Adventures in the Aid Trade: Forty years practising development in forty countries* (2020) by Richard Holloway

Adventures in the Aid Trade *is a pre-retirement memoir that traces 40 years of Richard Holloway's life as an international development practitioner, and his practical/personal encounters across 40 different countries. Robert described it as 'a very readable and useful book' (pers. comm.) that stands alone for the extraordinary range of experience and insights it presents; he knows of no other book quite like it. Robert's and Richard's paths crossed several times over the years with Richard happily accessing Robert's workshops ('hand over the stick'!) and Richard bringing Robert up to date with his latest experiences.*

A development nomad describing his trajectory

Adventures in the Aid Trade stands alone for the extraordinary range of experience and insight it presents. I know of no other book quite like it. Over the past 50 years, from 1966 to 2019, Richard Holloway has worked in at least 40 countries. A few like him who have worked independently as freelance consultants mainly from the North could make similar claims, but he differs in having engaged for a matter of years living and working in several of them – 6 years in Bangladesh, 5 in Indonesia, 5 in Zambia, 5 in Malaysia and shorter but substantial periods in Nepal, Botswana, East Timor and elsewhere. And in Indonesia he became fluent in the national language.

The life experiences recounted and reflected on here have not been in the mainstream of any organisation. This has given him flexibility but also insecurity. It shines through that he has avoided the freelancer's trap of telling sponsors what it is known they want to hear. He has taken the opportunities offered by a range of funders of programmes in which he could live, work and contribute substantially without being a career employee. It is much to their credit that his funders have given him space to be transparently and revealingly honest. He does not hide things but lays them out. He is self-critical and consequently credible, adding so much to the value of this book and what we can learn from it.

For those from countries which are the subjects of chapters, and for those from other countries, there is here fascinating detail about the reality of conditions, cultures and relationships at various times in the past half century. It will endure as a valuable historical document presenting an outsider's view, rounded and given depth by including his own country, the UK, where he worked with a community organisation inspired by squatters.

This book is then far from being the superficial descriptions and reflections of the brief visitor. It is a rich harvest of the experience of someone who has been critically aware of the cognitive traps and biases to which development professionals are so widely vulnerable, and who has consistently and effectively striven to offset and avoid them.

In the course of his varied career, he has spent periods living and working in depth sometimes in remote areas and learning with and about poor and marginalised people. So these adventures are grounded in a remarkable and unique life experience, from which I and all other development professionals, and perhaps especially those setting out on hoped for careers in development, have much to learn.

This learning is made easier by Holloway's transparent honesty. This is a book of warts and all. He sets an example by laying bare what he did, and what did not work as well as what did. He is reflective about his own life, identifying what has helped him towards doing and learning better. Of his time at LSE he writes 'having more field experience made my LSE experience more pertinent and valuable to me'. There is a lesson there both for those who convene and those who choose to take part in courses related to development.

There is much to learn also from the topics and themes that recur. Of these, let me single out the most prominent and significant. This is corruption. It stands out in most countries and many contexts. It is often pervasive in whole organisations and administrative systems whether in Africa or Asia. Holloway recounts resolute attempts to overcome it, and its maddening resilience. It is not all gloom and doom though. There are successes and examples of what can work to diminish corruption and other malpractices. He works with advocacy organisations, and programmes of social accountability to enable people to claim their rights. He is involved in a repertoire of approaches which can be mobilised such as role plays, comic strips and cartoons. These are examples of the many practical experience-based ideas with which the book is replete and from which there is much to learn.

Perhaps most useful of all, and presented in a succinct and accessible form, are the concluding sections in almost every chapter entitled 'What did I learn at the coal face?' Here is well grounded advice which gives scope for much reflection, internalisation and action. Taken together, these sections present a wise and informed source, to influence one's choices and decisions. These short sections are a treasure trove for all of us from all countries, North and South, in the spirit of universalism of the SDGs, whether we are freelance or work in governments, CSOs, the private sector, the media, academia, or specialised professions. It is for all of us who are eager to learn practical lessons and to improve our practice.

Looking to the future, Holloway starts with the present. He notes the increasing commercialisation of aid, and the top-down accountability, and the market language that go with this, and with the large consultancy firms that receive big contracts. The phrase 'the aid trade,' represents not so much cynicism as realism about currently prevailing aid transactions and relationships. Throughout the book his optimism and positive attitudes and approach shine through. It is the same with the future. He recognises that we are in a new space. The future will not be like the past. We live in a new enthralling post-post-colonial world of peers, mutual accountability, and co-learning for which he was a pioneer ahead of his time.

For all who work in development or aspire to do so, *Adventures* is a grounded and invaluable source of learning and inspiration. It is a rich source of ideas for how we can do better. I commend it to all development professionals, whatever their roles, as an engaging read and a fertile source of learning.

Source: Holloway, R. (2020). Adventures in the Aid Trade: Forty Years Practising Development in Forty Countries. Abingdon: Routledge.

Reflections from Richard Holloway

As he worked for CSOs around the world as a development practitioner, Richard would intermittently bump into Robert as he offered a workshop, and seek to join. He took Robert's thinking on board as he gradually moved through the roles of field volunteer, CSO programme coordinator, project manager, then programme director for national or international donor organizations. This continued as he became a field volunteer again, conducted his own writing and training; they would meet, re-meet and discuss. Robert agreed to 'Foreword' Richard's pre-retirement memoir Adventures in the Aid Trade, *showing once more his sharp insights into the development trade.*

Calling your book *Forty years practising development in forty countries* sets one up for ridicule, or at least tolerant scepticism. Can the experiences of one man in development still be pertinent after so many years, particularly when he was itinerant, contributing to many organizations (although not leading any)? Can this be true even when Robert's on your side and batting for you?

Robert's endorsement of what I wrote in my book (*Adventures in the Aid Trade* – Routledge 2020), and what I recounted there, was hugely satisfying to me – allowing me to feel that indeed I had something worthwhile to say, and that others might well have something to learn from my experiences and thinking. Robert's readiness to lend me his reputation was tremendous – I no longer had to be apprehensive about the value of what I was saying, no longer so ready to duck accusations of missing the big policy implications of suggested development interventions.

I did not have to be cautious about saying: Yes, appropriate technology is still relevant; yes, paying for education through production still makes sense; yes, positive deviance is still being ignored; yes, building integrity is needed to balance fighting corruption; yes, CSOs do have much to offer, if only governments and donors would work honestly with them. To have these ideas called 'treasure troves' for 'all of us who are eager to learn practical lessons and to improve our practice' was inspiring. This might lead somewhere… and give validity to 40 years' work.

However, this does not seem to have led anywhere: the lockdown of universities over Covid did not help, but my expectations that the topic, the publisher, and Robert's reputation (and endorsement) would suggest the value of the book to those who 'work in development or aspire to do so' and to those who train others in that field, has not come about. I don't know of people or institutions that are using the book and what Robert calls 'the well-grounded advice'.

Perhaps our aim is wrong. Who trains the next generation of development practitioners? If universities, then perhaps the need for theory has taken undue precedence over practice; if development agencies, then perhaps the importance of raising money has taken over from building the quality of delivery; if CSOs, then perhaps they don't expect to have to do their own training.

So, Robert's foreword has informed me that I have been on the right track, and his large experience tells me that I have something useful to say to and for development co-practitioners. If I had not had that endorsement, I would not be writing this. But the rush to use these ideas has been under-whelming to say the least. Perhaps this book will encourage a moving forward that includes with it a critical appreciation of what has been learned before.

Failing forwards

Tessa Lewin

(Distilled musings from my conversations with Robert while compiling this book)

Robert often characterizes himself as 'failing forwards'; in fact, it is something he celebrates. Implicit in 'failing forwards' is the recognition that the necessity to act carries with it the inevitable risk of error; a risk that must be embraced if we are to learn, and to achieve the 'good change' that is Robert's capacious definition of development. And crucially, a risk that must not be used as an excuse for paralysis (Brydon-Miller, 2004: 13). Apparently, we have Robert's failure as a manager to thank for these forewords. He claims to have been a top-down and ignorant manager, one whose arrogance was a disability. One might argue that this realization (and Robert's unusual capacity to accept it) ushered in a useful humility, and a career-long awareness of the need for careful reflexivity, to proactively overcome inevitable blind spots and biases; and an enthusiastic willingness to contest orthodoxies and challenge hierarchies.

Indeed, we might also celebrate his failure as a certain type of academic. Robert insists that he has only ever been a trainer-facilitator because he does not know enough about any particular subject to teach it. He talks also of the shame, frustration, and anger he felt when he was turned down for promotion by the IDS appointment committee, one member of which kept asking him about recent developments on the subject of his doctoral thesis, settlement schemes in tropical Africa, a subject on which Robert was no longer working. He describes this rejection as a gift, one that motivated the continuation of his nomadic lifestyle, full of the advantages of not being trapped in a particular discipline. This 'failing forwards' afforded his valuable positionality as strategic outsider; it allowed him to pay attention to the margins, to the 'cracks' between disciplines, where much of the knowledge pertinent to building a better world was to be found. His un-disciplined career served also to nurture his capacity for agile opportunism.

Both Robert's outsider positionality, and his agile opportunism, are evidenced in the collection of work here which, despite its magpie veneer, exhibits an eclectic coherence. All the publications are in some way concerned with 'good change', or as the two of us suggested some time ago 'inclusive universal justice' (Chambers and Lewin, 2020). As such, they are all also concerned with either 'knowing better', or 'doing better'.

Knowing better

> *'the truth is rarely pure, and never simple'* – Oscar Wilde

Robert often commented that it would be wonderful if there were more people who cared passionately about reality, and about understanding reality. Much of the work he has written forewords to is concerned with the struggle to better access the truth of complex situations; of migrants, of poor people, of children, of those structurally marginalized and excluded by existing social hierarchies. It is also about questioning the mindsets and attitudes underpinning these exclusions, which consciously or unconsciously are racist, gender insensitive, neo-colonial, anti-democratic, or exclusionary.

He has written about the exhilarating moment when he realized that talking to local farmers could yield richer, more accurate, more timely insights than those afforded by large-scale 'scientific' surveys. He has championed work on immersion (Chambers, 2017; Jupp, 2021), that exposed policy-makers to the grounded realities of the contexts their work impacted. He has argued for research processes that allow for emergence, and with it, the potential disruption of prior knowledge and overly simplistic perceptions; and for approaches that take adequate account of complexity. His proactive and life-long searching for what he calls 'methodological win–wins', suggests that we should seek to know better by all means possible.

Robert and I had many conversations about the internet, particularly about the early optimism that it would facilitate better access to multiple realities and expose us to different views. Sadly, this was fast eclipsed by a recognition of social media's capacity to propagate the mis- and disinformation that, in many ways, has made the truth more elusive than ever. The proliferation of fake news has coincided with a loss of trust in the traditional institutions of government and mainstream media. In this context, listening to trusted people who are impacted by policy decisions, through careful, local, and participatory research, is more important than ever.

Given the high levels of political polarization currently evident, so too is an embrace and articulation of nuance and complexity. Grant (2021: 165), writing about 'binary bias', a tendency to simplify 'a complex continuum into two categories', suggests that 'we can learn to recognise complexity as a signal of credibility' (Grant, 2021: 171), and 'favour content and sources that present many sides of an issue rather than just one or two' (ibid.). He also suggests that we train ourselves (and others) to always ask 'how do you know?', both of ourselves and of others (Grant, 2021: 211), as a reflex for precisely the standard of rigour called for by many that have contributed to this book.

Doing better – towards radical equality

> *The word 'love' is most often defined as a noun, yet all the more astute theorists of love acknowledge that we would all love better if we used it as a verb* (hooks, 1999: 4).

Of course, knowing better is not enough, we need also to act. Covid and climate change have made highly visible the growing wealth gaps and damaging social hierarchies we inhabit, and the urgent need to move towards a more 'radical equality' (Butler, 2020) that recognizes our mutual interdependencies, both with other people, and the natural world.

bell hooks' writing on love acknowledges the careful, intentional, daily labour required to first establish, and then maintain, functional architectures of care. It is this care-ful ethic that we need to cultivate as development thinkers and practitioners.

International development carries the significant historical baggage of the 'us-them' relationships, complicit in the exploitations of racial capitalism. But also, within it, is a long history of support for social justice movements, for relationships of solidarity and sustainability. The work that Robert champions here, sits within this tradition of Development as 'good social change'. It is about listening to the margins and working proactively towards a radical social justice and inclusion; about challenging and holding to account those who perpetuate unequal arrangements of power. It is about working to dismantle the violent and damaging hierarchies of class, caste, abilities, race, gender, sexuality, and age. It is a development built on the understanding that each life has value, and that all of us have a responsibility, and the capacity, to do better.

As we continue to fail forwards, we hope some of the reflections in this book will be thought-provoking and useful to inspire ambitious attempts to do better – a development concerned not just with surviving, but with thriving.

References

Butler, J. (2020). *The Force of Nonviolence: An Ethico-political Bind.* London: Verso.

Brydon-Miller, M. (2004). 'The terrifying truth: Interrogating systems of power and privilege and choosing to act'. In Brydon-Miller, M., Maguire, P. and McIntyre, A. (eds.), *Traveling Companions: Feminism, teaching, and action research*, pp. 3–19. Westport, CT: Greenwood Press.

Chambers, R. (2017). *Can We Know Better? Reflections for Development.* Rugby: Practical Action Publishing.

Chambers, R. and Lewin, T. (2020). *Universal justice: a provocation* IDS Blog, 19 October. Available at: https://www.ids.ac.uk/opinions/universal-justice-a-provocation/ [Accessed 3 October 2023].

Grant, A. (2021). *Think Again: The Power of Knowing What You Don't Know.* New York: Random House.

hooks, b. (1999). *All About Love: New Visions.* New York: HarperCollins.

Jupp, D. (2021). 'Using immersion research and people-driven design to improve behaviour change programs'. *International Journal of Market Research*, 63(1): 9–14. https://doi.org/10.1177/1470785320980631

www.ingramcontent.com/pod-product-compliance
Ingram Content Group UK Ltd.
Pitfield, Milton Keynes, MK11 3LW, UK
UKHW060455150426
5217IPUK00027B/2077